Telling Tales

Telling Tales: Making Sense of Christian and Judaic Nonsense

The Urgency and Basis for Judeo-Christian Dialogue

Jacob Neusner

Westminster/John Knox Press
Louisville, Kentucky

Scripture quotations from the New Testament are from the Revised Standard Version of the Bible, copyright 1946, 1952, © 1971, 1973 by the Division of Christian Education of the National Council of the Churches of Christ in the U.S.A., and are used by permission.

Translations of rabbinic literature are the author's own, except where otherwise noted.

Copyrighted material is credited as follows:

Haim Hillel Ben-Sasson, "Disputations and Polemics," *Encyclopedia Judaica* (Jerusalem, 1971: Keter Publishing House Ltd.), 6:100–101. Used by permission.

George F. Moore, "Christian Writers on Judaism," *Harvard Theological Review* 14 (1921). Copyright 1921 by the President and Fellows of Harvard College. Reprinted by permission.

Hyam Maccoby, ed., *Judaism on Trial: Jewish-Christian Disputations in the Middle Ages* (Rutherford, N.J.: Fairleigh Dickinson University Press, 1981). Used by permission of Oxford University Press.

Book design by Ken Taylor

First edition

This book is printed on acid-free paper that meets the American National Standards Institute Z39.48 standard. ∞

Published by Westminster/John Knox Press
Louisville, Kentucky

PRINTED IN THE UNITED STATES OF AMERICA
9   8   7   6   5   4   3   2   1

Library of Congress Cataloging-in-Publication Data

Neusner, Jacob, 1932–
    Telling tales : making sense of Christian and Judaic nonsense :
the urgency and basis for Judeo-Christian dialogue / Jacob Neusner.
    — 1st ed.
        p.   cm.
Includes bibliographical references and index.
ISBN 0-664-25371-7
    1. Judaism—Relations—Christianity.   2. Christianity and other religions—Judaism.   3. Judaism (Christian theology)   I. Title.
BM535.N385   1993
296.3'872—dc20   92-29802

Contents

Prologue

Part One

WHY THERE HAS BEEN NO JUDEO-CHRISTIAN DIALOGUE:
TWO MONOLOGUES AND THE CONSPIRACY OF HYPOCRITES

Part Two

TWO ISSUES FOR AN HONEST ARGUMENT
AND HOW THERE CAN BE A JUDEO-CHRISTIAN DIALOGUE

Part Three

UNDERTAKING DIALOGUE

Epilogue

Foreword

Author Jacob Neusner makes the astonishing claim that Judeo-Christian dialogue is nonexistent.

That claim seems to be refuted by the presence of lengthy lists of interfaith organizations, the countless posters advertising dialogue, and the numerous institutes devoted to improving Jewish-Christian relations.

On my shelves is a book-length bibliography of interfaith organizations from 1893 to 1979. It suggests that for precisely a century religious leaders and thinkers have created institutions for promoting dialogue. An entire chapter deals with "Christians and Jews: Overcoming Prejudice and Misunderstanding." One section lists "Inter-Faith in Israel" organizations. There are also "International Consultations," "Jewish Structures," dialogues promoted by the World Council of Churches and Roman Catholics. An appendix acquires the character of the telephone Yellow Pages, listing as it does many agencies which assure the future of dialogue.

Yet Professor Neusner contends that there has been no such dialogue, and that efforts to suggest it has gone on is "The Conspiracy of Hypocrites." He does not subtly whisper that charge. It appears in boldface type in a part heading and gets repeated through much of this book.

No dialogue? Even the term seems to have been resurrected for Jewish-Christian purposes. Until a few decades ago, dialogue was something actors had to memorize or scholars of Plato had to understand. Finally, in the twentieth century, people who were neither actors nor Platonists found good reasons to dust off the concept of dialogue and make it their own. One impulse was the very sincere, nonconspiratorial, nonhypocritical effort to face up to the horrors inflicted upon Jews in this century and to try to prevent even small replicas of these. Another impulse came with the Second Vatican Council, when Christians improved their ability to engage in "ecumenical conversation" while they needed a different term for talks between Christians and non-Christians, especially Jews. They could not say a creed together, as Christians could, but they could "dialogue." The third major impetus came from United States citizens of goodwill as they came to terms with a "post-Christian" and "pluralist" situation, in which Jews were the most visible non-Christian participants.

Despite all those impulses and energies, despite all the words spoken and the rivers of ink spilled, Rabbi Neusner insists that dialogue has not occurred, at least not dialogue that bears certain marks for which he is looking. Whatever else he might be accused of, no one can charge the author with being confused or oblique about his accusation that dialogue stopped after an event in Germany in 1933.

Since so many Jewish and Christian leaders and ordinary believers have a heavy investment in the dialogue they believe has occurred, since so many authors and publishers have issued books whose theses he has challenged, and since so many sincere citizens in general and people of faith among them in particular have heavy investments of hope in current strategies, Jacob Neusner stands a good chance of making new enemies with his charge. He had better be ready to defend his position. He is.

Before more than a page has passed, it becomes clear to the Christian reader that Neusner has no interest in attacking the Christian faith or Christians who profess it. This is not an assault on the integrity of Christianity but an attempt to have this integrity stand out as the author believes it cannot when dialogue with Jews leads to misdefinition of Christianity. I must say that often along the way I found him describing the central narrative or core convictions of Christianity more accurately from the outside than one often hears them confessed from within by over-obliging partners in dialogue.

Similarly, Neusner is not wavering in his own explicit attachment to the Jewish story and the faith it elicits and supports. It may be that no company of Orthodox, Conservative, or Reform Jews will turn to him to write statements of this story and this faith for the purposes of their organizations—though great numbers of them read him avidly and find his explications credible. But if he does not serve the organizations committed to dialogue in any direct sense, it is likely that his rather radical attempt at clarification will cause those who become aware of it to be more careful about their intentions in the future.

Is it Neusner's intention to tell others that, no matter how good their goodwill, they would do best to stop publishing bibliographies, starting institutes, supporting conferences, and talking, talking, talking? Not at all, though my "not at all" is only a three-word tease into the contents of the book. (I believe that writers of forewords are morally bound not to give the plot away or to overanticipate its turns.) Instead Neusner is saying that, far from the last word having been spoken in such dialogue—and, admit it, at times one wearies of the old form of such talk and yawns when invited to pursue it—the first words are only now being uttered.

Foreword writers are allowed to quote, however, and here is my quote from Neusner: "My proposal is very simple. When fundamental attitudes of the one toward the other shift, then theological solutions to the dilemma of Judeo-Christian dialogue will bring healing where there is no longer a wound. All things depend on attitude; proposition comes later, when it is scarcely needed, except for purposes of rationality." That word "attitude" could be misleading. Is the author turning sentimental on us, urging sensitivity training, "caring," and warm tingly feelings? Whoever believes that is the case has never read a page by Jacob Neusner. Attitudes based on such shallow and nonsubstantive approaches survive no tests and quickly change. This book is substantive. It suggests what both parties might do and say as first works and words when they undertake dialogue. If they are realistic, frank, aware of their own stories, they can further such dialogue. If they keep making up soft versions of their own traditions, they will produce mush or hypocrisy. They will waste everyone's time and create nothing but illusions.

On one level this book is a call for both broadly defined scriptural communities to go home and do their homework. Such study, such inquiry, such revisitation of one's own tradition is urgent and will never end, no matter how successful dialogue begins to be, no matter how much "healing where there is no longer a wound" occurs. But I read this also as an attempt to bring into focus not only the self and its community or tradition but the "other." One will need Christian spokespersons to write counterparts to this Jewish proposal. But for now, before the counterpart, we have the "part," by a Jew who knows how to get our attention and then, having gotten it, has something to say. Those who are convinced by the argument of this book will be more, not less, impelled to get dialogue under way.

MARTIN E. MARTY

Preface

After two thousand years of addressing one another through juxtaposed monologues, Judaism and Christianity are ready for dialogue, and in this book I explain how, while I hold there has never been a Judeo-Christian dialogue, I believe we can and should create one. I mean to write with candor and in a blunt way, but also in a fair and objective manner. A rabbi and a practicing Jew, I come to Christianity, both Roman Catholic and Protestant, with respect, just as, in my time, I have known many Christians, Roman Catholic and Protestant, who find in the Torah a valid religion on its own terms. No Christian should find in the pages of this book grounds for taking offense, nor should any Jew doubt my entire loyalty to the one God who gave the Torah to Israel, of whom, and with whom, I am one.

The urgency of dialogue flows from our shared professions: we believe in one God, who is the same God, who is the only God. Through the Torah have I learned something about that one God? Through Jesus Christ has my Christian neighbor and friend, in the society of open minds we share in this country, learned something about that same God? I find God in the Torah, my neighbor meets God in the person of Jesus Christ, and since we agree that we are speaking of the same God, we surely have something to teach one another and to learn from one another.

But until there is a dialogue, we are not going to find out what that might be. And even though a mighty industry, employing tens of thousands of people of goodwill throughout the world, pursues the work of Judeo-Christian dialogue, I do not think Christians respect the Torah, and I know that while Jews may find many nice things to say about Rabbi Jesus, the Galilean wonder-worker, they do not take very seriously Christians' conception of this man as God incarnate. I shall show that neither side has ever tried to make sense of the other in the other's terms, but I shall claim to propose some elementary steps that we may take, each in the direction of the other.

The reason the centuries have witnessed no dialogue—reasoned argument, based on commonly acknowledged facts, about propositions of mutual interest, exchanges of not merely opinion but reason, a "you" arguing with a "you"—requires little exposition. Dialogue was possible, since between Judaism and Christianity a vast, rich heritage of belief and sacred scripture is manifestly shared. Not only that, but since the first Christians were Jews, Christianity and Judaism stand in a special relationship. And, as a matter of fact, for nearly the whole of that history the relationship proved brutally honest in fact but profoundly dishonest in formulation. From the second century onward, Christians have formulated debates with Jews—as Justin with Trypho—or with Judaism, and, in the Middle Ages and modern times, Judaic theologians have participated, for their part, with a formulation of a debate with Christianity. But while going through the motions of argument and disputation, neither party brought to the debate the required attitude of reasoned disagreement about shared propositions among mutually respectful parties to discourse. No Judaic "you" ever argued with a Christian "you," but Judaic theological apologetics formulated an imaginary argument with a Christianity of their own invention, and Christian theological apologetics invented an equally fantastic Judaism. So much for the monologues—parallel lines that never met—that ran on in place of dialogue.

But each religion formed a doctrine of the other, one on the basis of which, to be sure, dialogue, or even genuine disputation, could never take shape. Christianity maintained that Judaism should have come to an end on the first Easter. Fulfilling the Torah, God's revelation to Israel at Mount Sinai, Jesus was, and is, Christ, the Messiah come to save the world. Judaism rejected him and his salvation. Therefore it was, and is, a false religion. Judaism held that Jesus was the illegitimate son of a Roman soldier, a mere magician, hardly the savior of the world. Christianity was, and is, a false religion. So, believing the other side hopelessly, invincibly perfidious, each party to the fictitious argument set forth its account of the other, self-evident in its sight, utterly implausible in the sight of the other. From the earliest Judeo-Christian dialogue through medieval times and down to the end of the nineteenth century the two faiths battled it out, each winning its argument of theological apologetics, neither ever really proposing to talk to the other anyhow. On that basis, over the centuries, the argument about who the true Israel is worked its way through the theological apologetics of both Judaism and Christianity.

But in modern times, and particularly since World War II, Christianity framed for itself a more benign account of Judaism, and Judaism of Jesus. So, people now suppose, a dialogue goes forward. Christianity affirmed the continuing validity of Israel's covenant with God. Israel, the Jewish people, was and remained God's first love. The Torah was, and is, a valid covenant for Israel. Judaism forms a valid covenant with God. Judaism for its part shaped for itself a Jesus to its own liking: a rabbi who said wonderful things with which Judaism can identify. Judaism then distinguishes the Jesus of history—who never imagined founding a new religion, Christianity, but only reforming the established one, Judaism—from the Christ of the church. The one, it honors and esteems: regards even as a prophet. The other, Judaism respects so far as it sustains the great teachings of Jesus. So Christianity was truly the continuant of Judaism, a religion to be respected and valued for bringing (much of) the Torah to the nations of the world. Jews then, and Judaism today, had every reason to honor and respect

Jesus, even though they did not join his followers in founding a new religion. So people now suppose there is a Judeo-Christian dialogue.

In the first part of this book I shall argue that that is not so, and in the second I shall explain how we may begin the very difficult task of making it so. Why do I maintain that the recent dialogue proves not much different from the received one of theological apologetics in the guise of interfaith debate? Until now, the well-meant formulation of that new relationship is not only disingenuous—each party struggling to find something good to say about the other—but, on the part of Judaism, false. The teachings of Jesus, measured by the criterion of the Torah that all Jews of his age, and all believers in Judaism to-day, believe God revealed to Moses at Mount Sinai, do not compel assent. So far as what he said conforms to the Torah, there is no reason to follow him in particular; everybody af-firms the same things. So far as what he said departs from the Torah, what he said and taught is to be rejected. And as a reformer of existing faults in Judaism, what Jesus said is either trivial or merely destructive.

These dissents to the insistence, "Sell all you have and follow me," concern not things Christians said about Jesus: for in-stance, the miracles he did, the rising from the dead to sit at the right hand of God, let alone the allegation that he was God in the form of a unique man. They concern what he himself is alleged by the Gospels to have said: the message he brought, in this world, to his own time and place. Whatever happened after he died is a matter of Christian faith. I see no basis for a forth-right dialogue with Christianity when Christianity is repre-sented as having come to an end the day Jesus died, and Jesus' never having risen from the dead. What I see is an adaptation of the figure of Jesus to a Christology acceptable to a Judaism, not Jesus Christ God, son of God, God incarnate. Why should Christianity conduct a dialogue that at the outset denies what makes Christianity Christian, which is Christ Jesus risen from the dead? I see no call at all.

On the Christian side, the description of a Judaism that was not supposed to have died on the first Easter, while rich in goodwill, turns out to look suspiciously like the Christianity of the theologian responsible for the description. Judaism (whether in the first century or in the twentieth) is, for instance, accused of being legalistic. But its latter-day apologists demonstrate that it really was not (so) legalistic, because its legalism formed an expression of the covenant with God, thus "covenantal nomism." Explaining legalism by explaining it away, the mainly Protestant defense of Judaism validates the faith by claiming it conforms to Protestant norms. That may serve for Reform Judaism, but it hardly forms a profoundly appreciated defense of a Judaism that encompasses dietary laws, Sabbath and festival observance, and a way of life affecting many corners of human existence treated by Protestant Christianity as neutral. Why should any Judaism conduct a dialogue that at the outset denies the Torah's holiness, affirming only those aspects of the Torah that conform to someone else's notion of what God can talk about anyhow?

Given the clumsy and inexperienced ways in which Judaism and Christianity alike, up to now innocents, even virgins, to dialogue, have attempted to approach one another, we must wonder, Why seek dialogue now? The systematic murder of nearly six million Jews in Christian Europe provides the answer: not collective guilt, which Israel, accused of collective murder ("deicide") for centuries, cannot now impute to others, but, it is clear, collective shame. Many recognize that Christianity's teaching of contempt created the attitudes that made the Holocaust not only possible but plausible and, under the right conditions, inevitable. From "You may not live among us except as Christians" (as a German theologian told Martin Buber on the eve of the Holocaust), it was not a giant step to the view, "You may not live among us," and then, "You may not live." Many took that step: German guards sang Christmas carols in Auschwitz, and—I think, in consequence—Christianity in many forms has acknowledged its share of collective shame. From Vatican II onward, important Christianities have formulated a theologically valid Christian alternative to a teaching of contempt. These make possible a Judeo-Christian dialogue. But no one yet knows what form it is to take.

So too, in response to gestures of reconciliation, Judaism's position of implacable rejection awaits modification, adaptation to facts never before encountered among Christianities. How, though, are faithful Jews going to acknowledge the existence of Christianity after two thousand years of pretense that in the person of Jesus and the formation of Christian churches nothing has changed and nothing has mattered?

Answers to these difficult questions will not arise easily, but in these pages I suggest ways of seeking them. Up to now people have moved too far, too fast, promising too much. So we have asked ourselves not to make some sense of the other in our own terms but, rather, to acknowledge the other in the other's terms. On the part of Judaic theologians of Christianity, Judaism moves toward a position of affirming Christianity for everybody but us. And, on the Christian side, major church bodies have affirmed that Israel comes to God through the Torah and have treated as enduring, even after Calvary, Israel's eternal covenant with God—Israel after the flesh. These theological initiatives, tentative and occasional as they presently appear to be, introduce a certain implausible quality to the dialogue; we Jews find ourselves saying something we have never before conceded, and I think the Christians locate themselves in an equally unfamiliar circumstance. Matters have moved too fast, and in the wrong direction. I propose here to lead in a direction not yet explored, in common or severally, by Christianity and Judaism.

My basic contribution is to suggest a different way in which each may think about the other, one that, at this early stage in the nascent dialogue, asks for not theological affirmation—which, given altogether too facilely, changes everything but attitudes—but, rather, only a measure of sympathy. I really do not believe that Christianity is a true religion for the gentiles, because I do not believe it is true for us, Israel. I want no less for everybody than what God has given me, which is the Torah. But then can I, in my terms as a faithful Jew, form a sympathy for Christianity in its terms, so that the things it holds true strike me as other than implausible nonsense? When I can, then I have the right to enter into dialogue with Christians about Christ and also about the Torah. Sympathy comes first, perhaps then even empathy—both concerns of attitude, considerations of an honest conscience.

It is the simple fact that generations of Jews, down to my own mother, spoke about Jesus as Yoshke Pandra, little Joshua, the illegitimate son of the Roman soldier Pantera. So did the scurrilous *Toledot Yeshu* come to me; but my children have heard no such talk from me. Through my life and career, I have known more than a few faithful Christians, both Protestants and Roman Catholics, who may have heard about us as Christ-killers, or money-grubbing, or a bit sharp, but whose children have not—at least, not from their parents. My generation undertakes the welcome task of understanding what Christianity means when it speaks of Jesus Christ, God incarnate. Only when out of the resources of the Torah I can entertain in a sympathetic way in general what I now find nonsense both in general and in particular—Can anyone be God incarnate? Is this Jesus Christ God incarnate?—am I ready honestly to claim to be able to talk out of the resources of the Torah about Christianity. And Christians can readily translate these same profound dilemmas into Christian language, as I shall suggest in due course.

My proposal is very simple. When fundamental attitudes of the one toward the other shift, then theological solutions to the dilemma of Judeo-Christian dialogue will bring healing where there is no longer a wound. All things depend on attitude; proposition comes later, when it is scarcely needed, except for purposes of rationality.

Writing as a practicing Jew, I come to Christian readers with respect for them and their religion; not a line, not a word in these pages is intended to elicit a response of shame or guilt, though I speak bluntly and to the point throughout. My goal is to outline a way of thinking for Judaism, within the Torah, about Christianity, and for Christianity, out of the resources of Christianity, about Judaism: not to negotiate difference, surely not to accomplish a bloodless circumcision ("spiritually we are all Semites") or a dry baptism ("the best Christian among us is the Jew") and similar dissimulations, evasions, and hypocrisies.

To accomplish that goal, I have written, so far as I can, in a manner believers may find honorable, reasonable, and respectful. Where I have not achieved that goal, I do not defend, but in advance express regret for, my failure or error.

This book forms the third of four works on Judaism and Christianity in dialogue: *Jews and Christians: The Myth of a Common Tradition* (New York and London: Trinity Press International and SCM Press, 1990), and *The Bible and Us: A Priest and a Rabbi Read the Scriptures Together,* with Andrew M. Greeley (New York: Warner Books, 1990). The former argues that there is not now and never has been a "Judeo-Christian tradition." The latter maintains that Judaism and Christianity do not even share scriptures in common, since Judaism reads the Torah in a manner entirely different from the way Christianity reads the Bible. In the fourth part I argue with Jesus: a gesture of respect. This is *A Rabbi Talks with Jesus* (New York: Doubleday, 1993). Having raised the question of Judeo-Christian difference, I here wish to suggest a means not of obscuring difference, surely not of negotiating theological truth, giving a bit and taking a bit, but rather finding a way of making sense of the other party's nonsense: a small beginning.

Prologue

1
Time to Talk

As Christianity reaches its two thousandth birthday, the state of the world presents an opportunity for which religious people have waited since the Enlightenment and the nineteenth-century pronouncement that God is dead. True, gods have died. But Christians, Muslims, and Jews know that our God—the God of Abraham, Isaac, and Jacob, whom Judaism proclaimed and Christianity and Islam brought throughout the world—rules. The gods that reigned for the final centuries of the second millennium now pass. Communism has died. Bare, ruined choirs in Russia get roofs. Europe has completed its century of civil war. Nationalism is discredited as ancient peoples, submerged within nations and denied even their own language, now find their voice. And as to telling people how to live, calls to define one's life around the service of the nation embarrass—or merely amuse. Indeed, few find final solutions in politics at all to tough questions of human existence. And as to accounting for the social order and setting forth the social compact, reasons of state and nation seldom persuade.

Indeed, when people ask why they live and what they are meant to do together, in the lands where Christianity and Islam have taken root, people turn to Christianity and Islam who once turned to communism or nationalism. Not only so, but in

Christian lands people ask Christianity to teach them how to reconstruct the social order, and Islamic nations—Malaya, Pakistan, Iran, much of the Arab world—turn to the idea of the Islamic state and society in shaping the politics of the hour. These are remarkable events, showing Christendom and Islam to be not the receding tide of the past but the wave of the future, overwhelming the politics of atheism and communism that, in their day, announced religion's doom. And, where people these days turn away from Christianity or Islam, it is to transient things, which cannot long sustain: when people have pretty much everything they want, they will find, as have much of the West and the world for a long time, everything you want is not enough. The hour of religion strikes once more: no longer to call to an age of faith, to be sure, but at least to remind an age of little faith that God awaits. I do not think the next hundred years will witness the start of many cathedrals. But I doubt many churches, mosques, and synagogues will close for lack of the faithful.

So if Islam, Judaism, and Christianity meet an oncoming world, these world-ruling faiths, for their part, also stand at the turning of the tide. The great faiths stood on the defensive for this century and the one before. They have survived. They have endured. They have not lost their voice. In the age now closing, the faiths faced within, turning a hard crust to the world beyond; today, it is clear, Christianity has chosen to reach out to Judaism, and the Christian West would enter discourse with Islam as well. Now established in its holy land, the Land of Israel, and secure in the western democracies as well, Judaism too engages on their own terms issues of religious dialogue that, for two hundred years, were addressed in a merely politic manner. Whether or not Islam—Indonesian or Malayan or Pakistani, or Iranian or Egyptian and Moroccan and Tunisian—finds itself ready to talk as it did so masterfully in its philosophical centuries no one now knows. But, it is clear, a long era in the relationships between and among Christianity, Judaism, and Islam has now closed. A new era awaits us all. We may be able, ourselves, to decide what it shall be.

The age now closed is one in which either Islam stood on the defensive, or went over to the attack, or Christianity attacked or struggled to hold its own. Now, perhaps for a brief moment, perhaps for a long time, the great world-shaping, world-girdling faiths stand poised for we know not what, but none now attacks, and no one need mount a defense either. For its entire history, Islam has found itself confronted by Christianity; and from the birth of Islam, the history of the West has narrated the tale of the struggle of Christianity to hold, then force back, Islam, and then to hold again and force back again. First came the struggle with Arabic Islam. From Tours and Charles Martel in 732 to the first Crusade in 1096, Christianity defended against Muslim attack. It lost its Holy Land and historical center, in the Near East and North Africa; it gave up Spain. With Spain reconquered in 1492, Christianity turned to the Far West.

But even then Middle and Eastern Europe undertook its struggle with Islam, now against Turkish Islam, which completed the conquest of Christian Asia Minor, in 1453, and took Greece and Macedonia, moving north and westward even to the gates of Vienna itself, in 1672, and receding only a little afterward; and the best energies of Middle and Eastern Europe were required to hold Vienna itself. But Islam fell back—with the Dutch in Indonesia; the British in Malaya, the Indian subcontinent, and the Near and Middle East, Egypt, and the Sudan; the British and Russians in Iran; the Russians throughout Muslim Central Asia; and the French in Muslim Africa, Tunisia, Algeria, and Morocco. The age of imperialism marked the final western and Christian offensive, with Islam on the defensive from its heartland to its western- and easternmost antipodes. Few Muslim states ruled themselves; many were incorporated into imperial Christendom. But the imperial age has ended; much of Islam is governed by Muslim states, and Christendom outside of Europe no longer rules.

None now confronts sustained aggression, and no one now means to do more than hold things as they are. What tomorrow will bring in the thirteen-hundred-year competition between Christian and Islam—the monotheist civil war—we can scarcely foresee. One tide has run its course, another not commenced. Tides go out, tides flow in. For a brief moment, the waters mill about, too late to flow out to sea, too soon to shift toward shore. So too, it is ebb tide in world history, the Christian and the Muslim. Christendom does not defend against Islam. But it no longer attacks. Islam no longer defends, but has yet to take the offensive. And that is so not only in the politics of empires and nations.

Nor does the common enemy, militant secularism, now mount a sustained successful offensive against either Islam or Christianity or Judaism. In the Muslim lands, no one today believes Islam loses out, not to Christianity, not to communism, not to secularization. And in countries where Christianity forms a principal means of defining the social order, the wave of the future no longer is seen to flow toward a secular world, but many, the Communist god having failed, now make their way to long-closed, long-ago-desecrated churches.

Judaism, for its part, has come to the end of one story and stands well beyond the prologue of another, and unanticipated, one. Standing at the threshold of the now-dying century, who would have predicted that where Jews then lived no Jews would live; but where then few Jews lived, Judaism would take root. In 1900 a vast ocean of Jews flourished in the countries of Middle and Eastern Europe; today memorial stones mark the end of an entire civilization, its people and its languages. In 1900 a handful of Jews began to build a Jewish state in the Land of Israel, and many more fled westward to the Americas. At that moment of mass migration, no one knew what would come of Judaism in the western lands where Jews found refuge and hope for themselves. Many, in the countries of migration, believed that in America one could not live a Jewish life, but they went off anyhow. And—to mark the unanticipated in its truly somber color—who would have supposed that, midway through the century, most of the Jews of Europe, and Judaism in Europe, would perish?

But, too, who would have imagined, in the maelstrom of annihilation, that in a brief moment a Jewish state would reestablish itself in the Land of Israel and that the word "Israel" would speak not of a holy, otherworldly religious entity, the holy people, God's first love, but of a state and a homeland? Given the then paramount movement among masses of Jews away from Judaism and toward a variety of other gods—socialism, for example—none could reasonably have anticipated that, on the eve of the twenty-first century, the single most powerful motive force for Israel, the Jewish people wherever they lived, as well as for the state of Israel, would be the religion: Judaism. But it is.

So the moment marked by the turning of the millennium surprises. Islam has not retreated before the inexorable forces of westernization, secularization, and Christianity. It has held its own. It has regained its central role in most Islamic countries. The world has now to reckon with Islam. Christianity has not fallen before communism, but communism before Christianity. Christianity has not passed into desuetude in many western countries—Germany, the United States, Canada, for instance—but finds a rebirth, whether in Roman Catholic or Orthodox or Protestant or Evangelical and Bible-believing form. Judaism, apparently losing its masses to other ideals altogether, whether to culture or to progress or to liberalism, finds its holy books once more much studied, its holy way of life again a vivid choice for holy Israel.

The world addressed by Islam, Christianity, and Judaism opens its ears. With people prepared to listen, long-held attitudes giving way, and politics and culture accessible in ways in which, for a long time, they were not, the one God of Abraham—speaking, in Christianity, through Jesus Christ God incarnate, in Islam through the Prophet and the Quran, and in Judaism through the Torah—may now find a hearing. Monotheism comes to a triumphant moment: it has survived, it has endured, it has kept the faith, it has a faith to set forth.

And yet—

And yet, if those great religions of the world, Christianity and Islam, find themselves once more at center stage, and Judaism along with them in the world it has chosen for itself, it means only that the world listens, an audience awaiting a new human drama. But will Christianity and Islam find words to say beyond the old familiar audience, believers who have heard the

words before, to an audience of unbelievers but also not scoff-
ers? For its part, will Judaism find a message to speak to a world
prepared to listen? No one now knows the answer to that question. The reason is simple. For the two thousand years now
drawing to a close for Christianity, no less than for the fourteen
hundred years of Islam, not to mention the fifty-seven hundred
years Judaism counts from the creation of the world as accounted for by the Torah, these three great religions have announced to humanity belief in one and the same God but have
found it exceedingly difficult to explain to one another anything about that one God whom all have known, whom all have
proclaimed, from Sinai, through Jesus Christ, through the seal
of the prophets, Muhammad.

So all have known that one God, whether in the person of
Jesus Christ, God incarnate, or in the revelation of the one
whole Torah given by God to Moses at Sinai, or in the Quran,
"the word of God in the strictest sense of the term—not only as
example and admonition but as a decree coming from the very
mouth of God."[1] But believing all in one and the same God,
appealing to one and the same story of creation, sharing in
common such prophets as Abraham and Moses, and revelation,
from Sinai and the prophets, like children of common parents
they sustained for most of their lives on earth a certain loathing
of one another, on the one side, and an utter incapacity to
communicate, on the other. So they have turned inward, each
talking to its own audience, none proposing to speak beyond its
own walls, except to explain to the others how misguided about
God they are. At best each has offered the outsiders tolerance,
bestowed perforce; at worst, a malign relativism—each is right
for its own—masked mutual incomprehension.

Whether even now one wishes to talk with another is not
altogether clear. But that the world will listen is beyond doubt.
For the time to talk has come, when each party has gained
something of what it has long wanted: Islam no longer under
the heel of Christian Europe and its far western provinces,

---

[1]Josef van Ess, "Teaching and 'Universities' in Medieval Islam," *Di-
ogenes* 1991, 150:66.

Christianity no longer beset in Europe itself by a well-entrenched and strong alternative in communism, Judaism no longer bereft of place, a social order to which it states the norm. Working out century-old problems at home—whether in the Near and Middle East, the part of the Indian subcontinent now Pakistan, Malaya, Indonesia, and Islamic sub-Saharan Africa, for Islam; or in Europe and the Americas, for Christianity; or in the ancient homeland, now the state of Israel, and North America and Western Europe, for Judaism—the three religions that call Abraham and Sarah father and mother find respite. And they can look beyond themselves.

As I said, what is here appears to present a remarkable opportunity. But for what? Judaism on its own makes no sense of Jesus Christ, God incarnate; Christianity, on its own, cannot grasp Israel, God's first love, in terms holy Israel can comprehend; and Islam, so far as we in the West can reckon, has yet to frame a theory of the other religions of the book in terms that do not condescend and demean. So if the moment presents its opportunity, it can only be to accomplish what at no prior hour, in no earlier circumstance, the faiths of the one God known through Abraham, the Torah, Christ, and the Prophet, respectively, achieved. And that is not so grand a thing as making sense of difference, understanding how one and the same God whom all of us worship and love and serve could have said so many contradictory things to those to whom, through Christ, Torah, and the Prophet, respectively, that one true God addressed humanity: church, Israel, Islam, respectively. Perhaps another age will work its way toward that deep question, beyond our searching out. For us, a great step forward will be the simple journey toward understanding: the possibility, even, of conversation. For a long time, and I think for all time, we three have not conversed at all. I think the times are such that the time has come to talk.

The first step clearly leads Judaism to undertake dialogue with Christianity, and Christianity with Judaism.[2] The reasons

---

[2] I see no possibility for a dialogue with Islam in our generation, because the political obstacles presently overwhelm. Perhaps in an-

are quite simple. The two faiths have lived side by side for two millennia. Jews find Christianity familiar, and in North America and parts of Europe, to Christians, Jews present a familiar face as well. More compelling reason derives from the Christian and Judaic appeal to one and the same scripture, known to Christianity as the Old Testament and to Judaism as the written Torah. And, of course, as everybody concedes, Christianity took shape among Jews and for a brief moment represented a Judaism among Judaisms. But these perfectly valid reasons to expect a mutual dialogue between Judaism and Christianity have yet to bring about authentic conversation. What dialogue took shape before our own day consisted of two self-serving monologues. Neither took a keen interest in the other; both found, in making up a message for the other, essentially an occasion for reaffirming the self. Neither, in point of fact, could make sense, in its terms, of the other—and neither tried.

A genuine argument requires that different people argue about the same thing, appeal to the same facts, invoke the same canons of thought and reasoned argument. So dialogue makes

---

other age we may replicate the conditions that, for a brief moment in medieval times, permitted Judaism, Christianity, and Islam to converse in peace. But then the three religions really knew one another and lived side by side, and today that is not the case; Islam no longer knows us—neither Judaism nor Christianity—and we do not know them. For dialogue to commence, there must be a community of shared experience. And for that same reason, I see a dialogue between Judaism and Christianity in the United States, Britain, and France, where there are large and self-respecting Jewish communities living side by side with Christians of intellect and goodwill; both sides can identify appropriate conversation partners. That is not so in Germany, where the Jewish community has no interest in dialogue with Christianity, and where the Christian community labors under very heavy burdens of memory and shame. It is not so in the state of Israel, where dialogue with Christianity pursues an agenda defined principally by Jewish, Judaic, and Israeli partners (ethnic, religious, and political), and where the necessary scholarly foundations have yet to be laid. Dialogue, to work, requires a certain intellectual vitality, which is lacking in Jerusalem, and an attitude of enlightened respect for other religions, which, in the Israeli case, does not at this time extend even to other Judaisms besides segregationist-Orthodox ones.

contradictory demands: (1) thinking about the other in one's own terms and yet (2) framing one's thought in terms that the other can also grasp. An authentic effort at mutual comprehension—leading even to understanding and respect at the deepest layers of consciousness—demands (1) making sense of the other in one's own framework, yet (2) making sense of the other so that the other will recognize that sense too. Obviously, that kind of thinking beyond the limits of oneself proves difficult even under the benign circumstances of discourse among relatives or friends. Among religions, it is much more difficult, since our religions—at least, Islam, Christianity, and Judaism—claim to know God through God's own revelation. So the same God who tells me and my Muslim friend not to eat pork or carrion also tells the Christian that food makes no difference, and the same God who tells the Roman Catholic Christian that Rome is the rock on which to build has told Islam about a different rock altogether. Clearly, the message is confused.

And yet we do worship one and the same God, each by its own admission, and we do value, among other scriptures, the same scriptures. Not only so, but, as I said, we three together—Islam, Judaism, Christianity—stand at the end of dreadful trials and look forward with well-founded confidence upon a world that will now hear us out and that asks us to answer questions long addressed to not heaven but earth. So if we speak intelligibly, if, even, we find some one thing to say together, we shall be heard where until now we have been dismissed or ignored. But for the moment nothing suggests we understand one another so well that we may talk together, and much shows we do not. Now, whether or not anyone has ever known how to think about the other in a way authentic to one's own viewpoint but also plausible to the other's self-understanding, not many until now have tried to find out. It is time to try to talk. And no two religions in history have found more in common about which to talk than Judaism and Christianity.

Part One

Why There Has Been No Judeo-Christian Dialogue: Two Monologues and the Conspiracy of Hypocrites

2

That There Has Been No Judeo-Christian Dialogue: The Last Judeo-Christian Dialogue, Germany, 1933

How do we know whether or not dialogue takes place? Three criteria dictate the answer: (1) each party proposes to take seriously the position of the other, (2) each party concedes the integrity of the other, and (3) each party accepts responsibility for the outcome of discussion: that is, remains open to the possibility of conceding the legitimacy of the other's viewpoint. These criteria have only rarely been met in the entire history of Christianity's theologians' address to Judaism and Judaism's theologians' address to Christianity.[1] In point of fact, when the

---

[1] I find in the "demonstrations" of the Syriac Christian bishop Aphrahat a genuine dialogue, based on shared facts—the Old Testament is cited, rarely the new; reasoned argument—a persistent effort to introduce the other side's viewpoint and to refute it within the premises of the other side; and even a tone and attitude of respect and dignity. In my presentation of Aphrahat's writings, I have shown how remarkable a figure he is (see my *Aphrahat and Judaism: The Christian-Jewish Argument in Fourth Century Iran*; Leiden: E. J. Brill, 1971). It should be noted that Aphrahat wrote to Christians who were a minority in the Iranian empire and who, further, were fairly suspect of sympathizing with the Roman, now Christian, enemy of Iran. The tone and character of his demonstrations strike me as truly unusual, and I know of no parallel in the Judeo-Christian dialogue of antiquity; no other Christian writer on Judaism approached the civility and rational-

representatives of the two religions wrote as though to the other, they turn out to have been speaking to their own communities, respectively: letters written to the outsider but sent home in self-addressed, stamped envelopes. Whether or not writers expected the outsider to respond to or even to read what was said in the letter hardly matters; only rarely did theologians write in such a way as to show they knew (or cared) what the outsider would grasp.[2] Judeo-Christian dialogue (or disputation; the word choice hardly matters) formed an exercise in inner-facing apologetics.

Judaic contributions to dialogue have served only to resist Christianity's insistence that the sole point worth discussing is why the Jews do not convert to Christianity; no Judaic participant in interreligious dialogue before modern times conceded that Christianity bore a legitimate relationship to God's revealed Torah; none imagined lending credence to anything the other said. So far as dialogue rests upon shared principles of reason and logic and a mutually accepted corpus of facts, Judaism has only episodically found itself a participant to dialogue.

And the same applies to Christianity, from its beginning to nearly our own day. All Christianity has asked Judaism is, Why have you not accepted Jesus Christ and so gone out of business? That Judaism sustained a distinctive covenant with God never, before this time, has entered the mind of Christianity; that Jews sincerely and honestly believe in and practice Judaism lies beyond the imagination of Christians, who see Jews as stubborn and perverse; and never did a Christian participant in dialogue suppose that the outcome of debate and discussion

---

ity of Aphrahat's writings, and there was no Judaic writer on Christianity in antiquity, at least none whose writings have survived.

[2] I do not make reference to the interreligious discourse of philosophers of religion of Judaic, Muslim, and Christian origin; they wrote for each other and draw upon a common and shared store of reason, logic, facts, and criteria for truth. At issue here is disputation and dialogue between believers and in the context of belief: theological dialogue and philosophical argument have to be carefully distinguished one from the other.

might encompass a change in attitude or viewpoint on the Christian side.

Not only so, but only rarely through time have theologians speaking for the two great traditions even addressed a common set of issues. I have argued[3] that in Judaic writings emerging from the fourth century—when Christianity became first a licit religion, then the established religion of the Roman empire— we find considerable interest in issues that Christianity addressed to Judaism. Specifically, a Christian agenda concerning the salvation of Israel and the coming of the Messiah ("the prophets' promises to Israel have now been kept, and Israel will not be saved except through Jesus Christ"), the status of "Israel after the flesh" ("the church is now the true Israel"), and the meaning of history from creation to then, seems to me to have found a counterpart agenda in Judaic writings. There we find an acute interest in the issues of when the Messiah will come, not critical in writings brought to closure prior to the fourth century; the genealogy of Israel after the flesh; and the periodization of history, with Rome the fourth and penultimate monarchy and Israel the ultimate. So far as a dialogue engages both parties in discussion of the same issues, the confluence of Christian and Judaic theologians' writings on a common set of topics, and their formulation of what is important about these topics into a single problematic, seems to me to point to the existence of dialogue.

And yet not a line in any Judaic writing that reached closure in the aftermath of the establishment of Christianity suggests that Christian propositions, Christian evidence, or Christian arguments were ever at issue. The Judaic documents took shape in sublime indifference to whatever their writers or compilers heard from Christianity, if anything. And from that time to the end of World War II, the two religions rarely even attempted to speak to a shared agenda. Conditions for debate later on did not accord equal standing to both sides. In no way can we

---

[3]In my *Judaism and Christianity in the Age of Constantine: Issues of the Initial Confrontation* (Chicago: University of Chicago Press, 1987).

characterize the discourse that took place from the fifth century to the twentieth as an interesting argument about issues important to each side, defined in the same way by each party to the discussion. Quite to the contrary, the issues facing the Judaic participants bore a political and not an intellectual character. The rights of Jews to live where and how they did were at stake in the disputations, whether medieval, whether modern; the beliefs of the Jews about the meaning and end of history, the Messiah in the end of days, and the definition of Israel scarcely came up. And when they did, Christians framed the issue, and Jews responded to the Christian framing of the issue: Why do you *not* believe? Nor, in their response, did the Jewish participants vastly improve on matters. They simply ridiculed the Christians' convictions: "They lacked both *ratio* and *auctoritas*," being devoid of scriptural foundation and without logical justification; so David Berger. No debate there, scarcely an intellectual confrontation.[4]

If, as I claim, the first implicit dialogue took place in the fourth century—and was reflected in fifth-century documents of Judaism—the next major intellectual confrontation, on the side of Judaism, took place eight hundred years later, in the twelfth century. Then the Christian side took the offensive, and, in Berger's judgment, "We find Jews arguing that Christianity is so inherently implausible that only the clearest biblical evidence could suffice to establish its validity." Issues of the initial confrontation scarcely occur in the medieval debates between Judaic and Christian officials, at least not in their classical formulation. An account of the disputations of the Middle Ages—Paris, 1240; Barcelona, 1263; and Tortosa, 1413–1414—therefore carries us into a world far removed from the one in which the issues of history, Messiah, and Israel pro-

---

[4]See David Berger, *The Jewish-Christian Debate in the High Middle Ages: A Critical Edict of the Nizzahon Vetus* (Philadelphia: Jewish Publication Society of America, 1979), p. 13. Cf. p. 11: "Christians were genuinely puzzled at the Jewish failure to accept the overwhelming array of scriptural arguments which they had marshalled."

duced a genuine confrontation on the same set of issues, defined in the same terms.[5]

Where there was dialogue, even in the form of a disputation, the sole reason for the Judaic participation was that theologians of Judaism were compelled to participate. So states the historian of the medieval dialogue, Hyam Maccoby: "The authority of the Inquisition did extend to some regulation of Judaism." The presence of kings and lords temporal as well as lords spiritual who bore considerable responsibility in public administration leaves no doubt on that score. When in the fourth century Judaic sages and Christian theologians constructed what I take to have been an argument, they addressed issues of mutual interest. The argument was joined fairly on matters of theological substance, each side working out its position free of the intervention of the other. But in the medieval disputations, Judaism stood in the dock, the accused. The charge for Paris in 1240 was that Judaism in the Talmud taught blasphemies against the Christian religion, made remarks against Christians, and revered holy books that contained unedifying material, such as nonsense or obscenity.

The issues at Barcelona in 1263 prove somewhat more interesting. Maccoby sees this as a debate rather than an inquisition. The Christian approach now was "to attempt to prove the truth of Christianity from the Jewish writings, including the Talmud." So Maccoby:

> Various Aggadic passages, collected from Talmud and Midrash, were thought to support Christian doctrines, especially the divinity of the Messiah, his suffering on the Cross, the date of his advent, and his promulgation of a new Law. Nahmanides immediately challenged the rationale of this contention.

---

[5]Twelfth century: Berger, p. 7, n. 2, "Anti-Christian works by Jews . . . are virtually nonexistent before the twelfth century"; Berger's judgment, p. 8.

In consequence of this approach, a further issue derived from the authority of the so-called Aggadic portions of the Talmud. The Judaic side treated the passages as unimportant, though the rabbis of the day revered them. Maccoby's judgment that there was a basic "lack of rapprochement and mutual understanding in the disputations" proves definitive: no argument here, only a confrontation lacking all shared discourse.[6]

As to Tortosa, 1413–1414, chaired by a pope and joined by representatives of the Jewish communities of Aragon and Catalonia, the disputation aimed at the conversion of the Jews.[7] Maccoby's judgment is this: "As far as the larger issues of Jewish-Christian confrontation were concerned, it added little to the Barcelona Disputation." But one thing is clear from Maccoby's fine summary: a matter of public policy greatly engaged the Judaic side: specifically, religious toleration. As one of the Jewish spokesmen stated:

> I say that all disputation about a principle of religion is prohibited, so that a man may not depart from the principles of his religion. It seems that only science should be made the subject of dispute and argument, but religion and belief ought to be consigned willingly to faith, not argument, so that he may not retreat from it.

Europe would have to endure the devastation, in the name of religion, of Germany and much else before even that much toleration might win support as a political policy, then in the form, after all, of *cuius regio eius religio*—not much toleration, but better than nothing. In any event the focus of discourse was this: "To prove the truth of Christian doctrines about the Messiah from certain passages in the Talmud." Judaic sages cannot have found very urgent the needs of such an agenda.[8]

---

[6]Hyam Maccoby, ed., *Judaism on Trial: Jewish-Christian Disputations in the Middle Ages* (Rutherford, N.J.: Fairleigh Dickinson University Press, 1981), pp. 11, 23, 26–38, 41–42.

[7]Maccoby, pp. 82–96.

[8]Maccoby, pp. 86, 89.

If there was a dialogue in the fourth century, it was because Christian theologians could consider in essentially the same terms as Judaic sages the scriptural issues they (correctly) deemed critical for Judaism. Aphrahat of course forms the exemplary figure, arguing so carefully on the basis of ancient Israelite writings when addressing contemporary Jews.[9] But I do not see the others as much different from Aphrahat. Eusebius addressed issues of world-historical interpretation, doing so in a rational and civil manner. Jerome wanted to engage in serious, equal argument with Jews, and so he took most seriously the lessons they had to teach—again, an encounter between equals. Chrysostom—alas! He did not argue as an equal to Judaic competition, but rather as a beleaguered and harassed figure, fearful of the future of Christians new to the church and impressed by the synagogue. Eusebius, Chrysostom, Aphrahat: each in his way addressed the other side by indirection, each with dignity, each in defense of the new faith.

Later on, when the encounter became not dialogue but disputation, a confrontation that was direct and provocative, it turned into a confrontation not between equals, not conducted with much dignity, and not aimed at clarifying, for the faith within, the issues of the challenge from the counterpart without. And this shift in tone and in substance, in the symbolic expression of the issues, expresses a more profound shift in the political realities that dictated and defined the terms of the tragic confrontation of the Middle Ages. In the fourth century, sages of Judaism could pretend to ignore the challenge of Christianity while at the same time systematically countering that challenge. Christian theologians forthrightly could enter the encounter with Judaism as with an equal. In the twelfth,

---

[9]This is Moore's judgment as well: "There is more reality in the homilies of Aphraates directed against the Jews . . . in the former we see that an aggressive Jewish polemic in the Persian Empire made necessary a vigorous defense" (George Foot Moore, "Christian Writers on Judaism," *Harvard Theological Review* 1922, 14:199). But Moore points out there were others of the same sort.

thirteenth, and fourteenth centuries, circumstances in no way afforded such an encounter.

A detailed survey of the successive cases in which Judaism and Christianity met head-on would change the picture in no detail. All that modern times contributed was a new form of Jew-hatred and Judaism-baiting, anti-Semitism, based on imputing to Jews for racial reasons despicable traits formerly assigned to Jews and Judaism by Christianity for only religious reasons. The Judeo-Christian dialogue of the twentieth century, until nearly our own time, provided Christianity with the opportunity to restate on both theological and racist grounds its case against not only Judaism but also the Jews. Then, in Germany in particular, the very willingness of Christianity to receive the Jews was claimed by Christian theologians to attest to the love and infinite grace of Christianity: it would accept the Jews despite their racially repulsive character. So Christianity made its own the racial anti-Semitism deriving from entirely secular sources.

A fine example of the union of theological anti-Judaism and racist anti-Semitism found entirely appropriate to interfaith dialogue derives from Eugen Rosenstock-Huessy, a Jew who converted to Christianity before World War I. In his correspondence during World War I with his cousin Franz Rosenzweig, Rosenstock-Huessy rang the changes on the themes of contempt, the loathing of Israel, the curse born by Jewry. Though both men fought for Germany and wrote under fire, Rosenstock-Huessy, born a Jew, wrote about the Jews and Judaism in Germany as alien and out of place, present only by reason of Christian condescension. Here is Rosenstock-Huessy, the Christian, addressing Judaism in dialogue:

> I know that Judea will outlive all 'the Nations,' but you have no capacity for theology, for inquiry after truth, or for beauty. Thou shalt not make any image. At this price the Eternal Jew may live because he hangs on tenaciously to the life granted to him.

Now Rosenstock-Huessy turns to the rehearsal of anti-Semitic stereotypes of the Jews as people without loyalty to their own countries, even, as I said, writing to a fellow German soldier, risking his life just as Rosenstock-Huessy risked his:

> But he is cursed to live by the sweat of his brow, taking loans everywhere, and making loans everywhere. The Jew dies for no fatherland and for no mission. He lives because his life does not approach the margin of life. He lives in a chimerical reflection of a real life that cannot be envisaged without the sacrifice of death and the nearness of the abyss. That Judea shall live on is dependent on the success of the individual Jew, on the number of his children. He is a paragraph of the law. . . . You do not know that the world is movement and change; the Christian says there is day and there is night, but you are so moonstruck that you think that the night view is the only view that exists, and you consider as the ideal conception the minimum of light, the night.[10]

Ben Sasson comments: "Rosenstock the apostate combines medieval Jew-hatred with the images of modern social and economic anti-Semitism. He considers that 'the emancipation of the Jews is a process of self-destruction for Europe.' "[11] German National Socialism, focusing upon the Jews as the source of all of the miseries that Germany had suffered and identifying the "extermination" of the Jews "like vermin" as the solution to the German problem, could not have phrased matters in a manner more suitable to its viewpoint.

No one should find surprising, therefore, that when the National Socialists did come to power, German Christianity found nothing to say to the Jews or to Judaism other than that despite the loathsome character of "the Jewish race," the Jews could still hope to experience the love and grace (and protection) of Christianity, if only they would convert. That no dialogue had ever taken place is best shown, therefore, by the final dialogue that did take place between Judaism and Christianity in Germany, before the destruction of the Jews and Judaism in Ger-

---

[10]Haim Hillel Ben Sasson, "Disputations and Polemics," *Encyclopaedia Judaica* (Jerusalem: Keter Publishing House, 1971), 6:99.
[11]Ibid.

many between 1933 and 1945. On January 14, 1933, the eve of
the National Socialists' rise to power, Karl Ludwig Schmidt,
meeting Martin Buber for the last disputation between German
Judaism and German Christianity, extended to Israel the invita-
tion to brotherhood with Christians—"but only as sons of a
Germany united through the Christian conception of the
Church as the spiritual Israel."[12]

The final voice of Christianity addressed to German and
European Jewry repeated the first and only message that
Christianity ever delivered to Judaism: "God has willed all this;
Jesus the Messiah rejected by his people, prophesied the destruction of Jerusalem. Jerusalem has been destroyed, so that
it will never again come under Jewish rule." A precursor of
the contemporary Christian judgment on Zionism, Schmidt
proceeds, "The modern world reacts to Zionism, which is national or even racist." He warns the Jews standing on the brink
of destruction that "the Church of Jesus Christ has again and
again shown her want of this Jewry, demonstrating her patience by waiting in hope that finally the Jews also . . . will be
able to perceive that only the Church of the Messiah, Jesus of
Nazareth, is the people of God, chosen by God, and that the
Jews should become incorporated in it, if they indeed feel
themselves as Israel."[13] So much for German Christianity,
fully aware of the coming triumph of National Socialism in
their country. For his part, Martin Buber answered in these
words:

> I live not far from the city of Worms, to which I am
> bound by tradition of my forefathers; and from time to time
> I go there. When I go, I first go to the cathedral. It is a
> visible harmony of members, a totality in which no part devi-
> ates from perfection. I walk about the cathedral with con-
> summate joy, gazing at it. Then I go over to the Jewish
> cemetery, consisting of crooked, cracked, shapeless, random
> stones. I station myself there, gaze upward from the jumble

---

[12]Ibid., cols. 100–101.
[13]Ibid., col. 101.

of a cemetery to that glorious harmony, and seem to be looking up from Israel to the Church. Below, there is no jot of form; there are only the stones and the dust lying beneath the stones. The dust is there, no matter how thinly scattered. There lies the corporeality of man, which has turned to this. There it is. There it is for me. There it is for me, not as corporeality within the space of this planet, but as corporeality in my own memory, far into the depths of history, as far back as Sinai.

I have stood there, have been united with the dust and through it with the Patriarchs. That is a memory of the transaction with God which is given to all Jews. From this the perfection of the Christian house of God cannot separate me; nothing can separate me from the sacred history of Israel.

I have stood there and have experienced everything myself; with all this death has confronted me, all the dust, all the ruin, all the world's misery is mine; but the covenant has not been withdrawn from me. I lie on the ground, like these stones. But it has not been withdrawn from me.

The cathedral is as it is, the cemetery is as it is. But nothing has been withdrawn from us."[14]

I am not certain what Buber means to say here. Is it "You're wrong, we're right"? Is it "You may be right, we may be right"? Or is it "Despite the grandeur of your cathedral and the mastery of the world it represents, we're right"? But whatever this fideistic exchange was meant to say, it certainly did not involve a confrontation with the explicit claim of the Christian conversation partner. Schmidt says that Israel becomes Israel only by accepting that Christ; Buber says what he says, but I see no response to that (to any faithful Jew, incomprehensible) claim at all. So no reasonable person, however sympathetic with Buber's situation, can find in these remarks a serious address to Christianity; all Buber finds to say is that, it is true, Christianity owns the world, but we are what we are: "nothing has

---

[14]Ibid., cols. 101–102.

been withdrawn from us." A dialogue should have required an address to the proposition, evidence, and argument of the other. But all Buber finds to say is: "You're wrong, we're right":

> We also know, as we know that there exists air that we take into our lungs, that there exists the plane on which we move; nay, deeper, more truly we know that world history has not yet been probed to its roots, that the world is not yet redeemed. We feel the unredeemability of the world. . . .
> There must be a nation in which the human answer can be fulfilled in life in its entirety, to which public life also belongs. Not the individual as an individual, but only the community as a plurality and unity, working together . . . can give God the full life-answer of man; therefore . . . there is Israel.

So the final message of Christianity before the destruction of European Jewry was that Jews can live in Europe only on acceptance of Christian terms: conversion. And the final response of Judaism was a simple denial. Perhaps Buber presented as his contribution to dialogue precisely what he thought Schmidt deserved: a reaffirmation of Israel, that alone. In context, that too constituted a considerable and courageous reply. But there was no dialogue between Schmidt and Buber, and, in light of what had gone before, there could not have been.

Ben Sasson comments, "Buber presents his thesis of open dialogue between Israel as a nation and religion and Christianity as a religion for other nations." Explaining how there can be both Judaism and Christianity in the world, Buber affirms:

> God's gates are open to all. The Christian need not come to them through Judaism. The Jew is not obliged to go to them through Christianity in order to arrive at God. . . .
> No man that is not of Israel understands the mystery of Israel, and no man that is not of Christianity understands the mystery of Christianity; but unknowingly they may ac-

knowledge each other in mystery. How it can be possible that mysteries exist alongside each other is God's mystery.

Again Ben Sasson: "With these words, Buber opened a way to divesting religious disputation of the polemical form it had assumed throughout most of its history. . . . Buber reformulated this conception in modern terms, where it assumes a validity through anguish that disregarded fear, facing danger and humiliation."[15]

No wonder that, at the end, Karl Ludwig Schmidt found no moral resources whatsoever upon which to draw a message appropriate to an ancient partner in argument. Even after World War II, when what Germany had done to the Jews was well known, German Christian theologians announced to the Jews that the murder of European Jewry constituted God's punishment of the Jews for not accepting Christ. Writing in "The Dean and the Chosen People," Richard L. Rubenstein points out that "the plain fact of the matter is that those who murdered the Jews were, if not believing communicants of the Christian faith, at least men and women whose only exposure to religion was derived from Christianity . . . men with university or professional training behind them. In some instances, former pastors were active leaders of the work of death."[16] Rubenstein tells the tale of a German pastor whom he met, who "looked at recent events from a thoroughly Biblical perspective. In the past the Jews had been smitten by Nebuchadnezzar and other 'rods of God's anger.' Hitler was simply another such rod." Such a position invites the conception put forth by the defense counsel of Adolf Eichmann, that "the death of the six million was part of a 'higher purpose,' and in recompense for an earlier and greater crime against God."[17] That response, seen by many as despicable, represented the perfectly reasonable conclusion for the Christian party to the dialogue to draw.

---

[15]Ibid., col. 102.

[16]Richard L. Rubenstein, *After Auschwitz: Radical Theology and Contemporary Judaism* (Indianapolis: Bobbs-Merrill Co., 1966), p. 47.

[17]Rubenstein, p. 55.

Through time, the Judeo-Christian dialogue provided Christians with the opportunity to express to Jews their loathing of Judaism and their contempt for Jews; the Jewish partner then found ready access to the high road. The partners to dialogue passed in the dark, going each in his own direction, scarcely aware of the other's presence, except in fantasy: a Jew who would find persuasive arguments in favor of Christianity in a parade of racist bigotry, a Christian who would find compelling a Judaic response framed in terms of God's mystery. So degraded a Jew, so disingenuous a Christian, never lived. Ben Sasson concludes:

> Jewish-Christian disputation thus began in the meeting of Justin and Tryphon under the shadow of the Bar Kokhba revolt. The darkness and flames of the Holocaust and the light from Zion may illumine the pilgrimage to ecumenical conversation on equal terms, toward understanding and harmonious living, waiting for God to solve his own mystery in history.[18]

So much for the last disputation before the end. Reading the terms of debate, we must affirm there has never been a dialogue. On terms such as these, in circumstances of impending doom, Christianity has nothing to say to Israel except, Accept Jesus Christ and then, but only then, shall we accept your humanity. Exceedingly harsh terms indeed, they marked the final chapter in a long story of Christian aggression and Judaic dissimulation, Christian insistence that Israel cease to be, Judaic evasions in appeal to God's mystery. Nor did the calamity of the German murder of millions of European Jews redefine the dialogue.

I myself heard the German theologian Wolfhart Pannenberg, at a Judeo-Christian dialogue at Harvard Divinity School in 1966, deliver precisely the same message that Rosenzweig heard from Rosenstock-Huessy and that Buber heard from Karl Ludwig Schmidt. The only question worth discussing, he maintained, is why Jews continue not to accept Jesus

---

[18]Ben Sasson, col. 102.

Christ—this under the auspices of the Harvard Divinity School and the American Jewish Committee. The death of nearly six million Jews had made no difference; what Schmidt said at the outset, Pannenberg said at the end. Nor is this position derived only from my memory; he wrote the same: "With the message of the resurrection . . . the foundations of the Jewish religion collapsed."[19] That there has been no Judeo-Christian dialogue requires no more sustained demonstration than the conception of the Rosenstock-Huessys, Schmidts, and Pannenbergs of what is appropriate and proper to say to faithful and believing Jews on the occasion of religious encounter. On the eve of the Holocaust, with the National Socialists assuming power, and just two decades after the Holocaust, with the moral standing and authority of Germany and German Christianity in ruins, Schmidt and Pannenberg addressed the same message to Israel. Can anyone wonder that, in his day, Buber simply said, We are what we are (he was too courteous to say, And you are what you are); and, in front of Pannenberg, some of us Jews laughed out loud?

Some dialogue! It was not even a disputation. Christian aggression, Judaic dissimulation—nothing more. Not only has there been no dialogue, there has not been even a moment of reflection on the requirements of dialogue, beginning, after all, with the condescension of courtesy—the condition of discourse, let alone dialogue, if anyone really wants to talk. What we shall now see is that neither Judaic nor Christian parties to dialogue have had any such intention. For each, dialogue provided the occasion of a monologue in affirmation of the faith. That is what I mean by "a conspiracy of hypocrites," the hypocrisy being the pretense that one wishes to conduct dialogue, the conspiracy being the agreement to pretend that matters of concern to the other party were at stake at all. Then what was at stake? The only open question is, Why should either party have taken the trouble to pretend to wish to talk with the other? Dialogue turns out to have served the quite autonomous

---

[19]Cited by Eugene Borowitz, *Contemporary Christologies: A Jewish Response* (New York: Paulist Press, 1980), p. 180.

requirements of theological apologetics, as we shall see in the answers to that question in the next two chapters, for Christianity and then Judaism, respectively.

3

The Judeo-Christian Dialogue as We Know It: The Christian Invention of "Judaism"

For the purposes of their own theological discourse, Christians first invented Judaism, then fabricated a dialogue with this Judaism, an imagined conversation with a made-up protagonist. Why, from the beginning, Christian writers wrote about outsiders, including Jews, requires no explanation. Every group defines itself by designating the other. Nor need we wonder why a Jew such as Saul, who first loathed, then loved, Christ Jesus, should have paid close attention to other Jews indifferent to the same. It was quite natural for him to want to define himself over against others of his same classification—Israel—who differed in that one critical way, hence to speak of an "us" both related to but different from "them," hence "the other Israel," "after the flesh."[1] Since earliest Christianity counted, among its enemies, Jews in command of synagogues, or Pharisees, scribes, Temple authorities, and the like, we hardly find surpris-

---

[1]That Paul refers to "Judaism" in this context need not detain us. "Israel" formed a generative category; "Judaism" ("Ioudaismos") occurs episodically and hardly defines a principal categorical problematic for Paul's thought. And the use of the peculiar "Judaizing," referring to people who circumcised their sons or refused to eat dead creeping things, has no bearing on the problem of this chapter.

ing that hostile Jews figure in a considerable account of "the Jews" in the Gospel According to John or the Temple authorities in Luke-Acts. Rubenstein proposes that "it may be impossible for Christians to remain Christians without regarding Jews in mythic, magic, and theological categories."[2]

If special attention to the Jews is natural, given the context of the Gospels' narratives, the formulation in Christian theological terms of "Judaism" is not. Indeed, what requires explanation is why a category, "Judaism," should have formed a medium for organizing data such that, if a writer invoked one component of "Judaism," all the other components of that same composite of beliefs and practices would come into play. And that is precisely how "Judaism" functioned as a category for Christian writers early and late. When people spoke of that -ism, and when they speak of it now, they have meant, and now mean, a well-composed structure of beliefs and practices, a religion, coherent (if not wholly uniform) among all its faithful: a homogenization of a variety of things into one thing. In the case of Judaism, they meant, and now mean, a religion that sets forth a variety of beliefs and practices, characteristic of all of those who profess said religion.

Now when we speak of that -ism, Judaism, we mean something other than what we mean when we talk of "the Jews," or

---

[2]Rubenstein states, "Jews alone of all the people in the world are regarded as actors and participants in the drama of sin and innocence, guilt and salvation, perdition and redemption. If the Jews are an utterly normal people like any other, capable of the same virtues and vices, then there is no reason to assert that Jesus had more than a human significance. The Christian Church must insist on the separate and special character of the Jewish people in order that its claims concerning the significance of Jesus may gain credence. As long as Jews are thought of as special and apart from mankind in general, they are going to be the object of both . . . abnormal demands and . . . decisive hatreds"; see Richard L. Rubenstein, *After Auschwitz: Radical Theology and Contemporary Judaism* (Indianapolis: Bobbs-Merrill Co., 1966), p. 56. One need not endorse this view of what Christianity must do in regard to Jewry in order to prove the truth of its beliefs about Jesus. But it does place the Christian half of the Judeo-Christian dialogue under a considerable burden.

"scribes, Pharisees, hypocrites," or the synagogue authorities. These form concrete, palpable social entities. In the case of "the Jews," John clearly means the enemies of Christ. When in the Passion narratives "the Jews" are portrayed as saying, "His blood upon our heads," a trait of that social entity, then and forever, is set forth: deicide. Attributing that trait to "the Jews" does not impute to all of them the same beliefs and practices: that is, an entire religion; it imputes one trait and that alone. When, by contrast, people make reference to "Judaism," they intend to claim that the religion characterizes all who profess that religion in one and the same way: a systematic corpus of ideas is held throughout, a cogent way of life (for instance, set of taboos) is observed. If, then, we know one thing, we know many more things; if we impute "Judaism" to a person, we know what that person believes, thinks, and does. By contrast, if all we say is that person is a Christ-killer ("his blood . . . "), we make a moral judgment but draw no conclusions as to matters not subject to discussion otherwise: what that person thinks, says, or does.

Now the notion of a systematic and cogent -ism, such as "Judaism," proves useful in describing a complex and diverse set of people; it simplifies the complexity, it covers over some of the diversity; forming a reliable common denominator, this "Judaism" sands down some of the knots in the wood. A philosophical way of thinking, defining an essence or delineating an idea that permeates the phenomena, the -ism-izing of a religion allows comparison and contrast and, in the theological framework, facilitates dialogue or disputation. In the pages you have already read, I have used the word "Judaism" countless times; we all do, all the time, along with Christianity, Islam, and the rest.

But in antiquity, the philosophical reading of a religion as an -ism competed with quite different ways of thinking, and while for Christian writers "Judaism" proved a critical category, for Jews, in particular in the Land of Israel, that -ism-izing of the things they believed and practiced represented an alien mode of thinking. "Judaism" presented for them no native category. When the Jews known to us from writings in Hebrew and Ara-

maic wished to speak in a cogent way about all the things they
believed and practiced, they used a symbol word, "the Torah."
If they wished to speak in a cogent manner about "what the
Jews believe and practice," they would frame their discourse in
quite different ways. Let me give two simple examples. If someone wanted to say who is a valid Israelite and who is not ("who
is in and who is out"), this is the language that would serve:

> All Israelites have a share in the world to come, as it is
> said, "Your people also shall be all righteous, they shall in-
> herit the land forever; the branch of my planting, the work
> of my hands, that I may be glorified" (Isaiah 60:21). And
> these are the ones who have no portion in the world to
> come: (1) He who says, the resurrection of the dead is a
> teaching which does not derive from the Torah, (2) and the
> Torah does not come from Heaven; and (3) an Epicurean
> [Mishnah Sanhedrin 10:1A-D].

What we have here is a perfectly straightforward answer to the
question "Who is Israel?" or, in contemporary language, "Who
is a Jew?" Now we are told what I must deny in order to be
excluded. Again, if someone wished to define the correct way
of life, what "Judaism" requires, there were systematic and or-
derly ways of presenting such a definition.

> A. R. Simelai expounded, "Six hundred and thirteen
> commandments were given to Moses, three hundred and
> sixty-five negative ones, corresponding to the number of
> the days of the solar year, and two hundred forty-eight posi-
> tive commandments, corresponding to the parts of man's
> body."
> B. "David came and reduced them to eleven: 'A Psalm
> of David: Lord, who shall sojourn in thy tabernacle, and who
> shall dwell in thy holy mountain? (i) He who walks uprightly
> and (ii) works righteousness and (iii) speaks truth in his heart
> and (iv) has no slander on his tongue and (v) does no evil to
> his fellow and (vi) does not take up a reproach against his
> neighbor, (vii) in whose eyes a vile person is despised but
> (viii) honors those who fear the Lord. (ix) He swears to his

own hurt and changes not. (x) He does not lend on interest. (xi) He does not take a bribe against the innocent' (Ps. 15)."

C.   "Isaiah came and reduced them to six: '(i) He who walks righteously and (ii) speaks uprightly, (iii) he who despises the gain of oppressions, (iv) shakes his hand from holding bribes, (v) stops his ear from hearing of blood and (vi) shuts his eyes from looking upon evil, he shall dwell on high' (Isa. 33:25–26)."

D.   "Micah came and reduced them to three: 'It has been told you, man, what is good, and what the Lord demands from you, (i) only to do justly and (ii) to love mercy, and (iii) to walk humbly before God' (Mic. 6:8)."

E.   "Isaiah again came and reduced them to two : 'Thus says the Lord, (i) Keep justice and (ii) do righteousness' (Isa. 56:1)."

F.   "Amos came and reduced them to a single one, as it is said, 'For thus says the Lord to the house of Israel. Seek Me and live.' "

G.   Objected R. Nahman bar Isaac, "Maybe the sense is, 'seek me' through the whole of the Torah?"

H.   "Habakkuk further came and based them on one, as it is said, 'But the righteous shall live by his faith' (Hab. 2:4)."

Bavli Makkot 24B

Here we have a fine definition of what, for the philosophical mind, would correspond to "Judaism," which is to say, a statement of the faith in a few straightforward and cogent sentences, the counterpart to "Judaism teaches," or "here are the essentials of Judaism," or "when the early Christians rejected Judaism, this is what they rejected."

But of course, that final option, which is a critical and urgent matter for the formulation of Christianity in its earliest phases, proves incongruent to the language of "All Israel" or "six hundred thirteen commandments." The reason is that "Judaism" forms an alien category, a way of thinking about something that, in the Israelite world, people who wrote in Hebrew or Aramaic did not think about; did not grasp; did not

set forth. Their modes of thought were not abstract but concrete, and while they answered questions of definition, the
questions were framed in a different language of thought, accounting, also, for the difference of the character of the answers. We recall, in this connection, the famous statement
attributed in a late rabbinic writing to Hillel, the first-century
sage, when asked to state "the entire Torah" while standing on
one foot: "What is hateful to yourself, do not do to your enemy; that is the entirety of the Torah; now go, study" (Babylonian Talmud Shabbat 31A). Clearly, "Judaism" forms no native
category; the native category that encompasses everything all
together and all at once is "the Torah."

When early Christianity wished to speak of the Israel that
had taken its own way forward, its repertoire ranged from
"brood of vipers" downward; we cannot expect Christian writers to speak of "the Torah" when addressing the beliefs and
practices of the other side. But nothing in the Gospels requires
invoking "Judaism" either, since, for the Evangelists, the enemies of Jesus Christ were persons, not abstractions: "scribes,
Pharisees, hypocrites," not an -ism. It is true that for the apostle Paul a different, more abstract mode of thought produced a
reference to that -ism, "Judaismos," which people reasonably
render as "Judaism."[3] By that usage, it is now clear, what
people intend is to say, "Judaism believes . . . Judaism practices. . . . " So if I know that someone is a Jew who professes
Judaism, then I know a great deal more about that person; and,
more to the point, I also am able to set forth that "Judaism" as
a coherent and systematic statement, which I am then able to
contrast and compare with "Christianity."

One problem in thinking in such a manner may be dismissed
as correct but trivial: in antiquity there was no such thing as a
single "Judaism," but there were many and diverse Judaisms.

---

[3]A wonderful and current account of the problem of defining "Ju-
daism" in the earliest Christian context is J. D. G. Dunn, *Partings of the
Ways Between Christianity and Judaism and Their Significance for the
Character of Christianity* (London: SCM Press; Philadelphia: Trinity
Press International, 1991), pp. 1–17.

Most people who have studied the matter now concur that we cannot speak of "Judaism" but only "Judaisms." But that fact of contemporary learning bears no consequences for our problem, since whether there was one Judaism or many, we still remain within the framework of a mode of thought that sets forth, for analytical and comparative purposes, a well-crafted set of beliefs and practices, subject to definition in the philosophical-theological terms that allow, also, for comparison with Christianity. And, it is clear, whether we compare "Judaism" to "Christianity" or "a Judaism" to "a Christianity" or "Judaisms" to "Christianities" hardly matters.[4]

A much more considerable problem in the -ism-izing of Judaism is that the very category, -ism, is invented for the purposes of dialogue with the -ism by the -ity that has invented the -ism. That is to say, Christianity, viewed by its writers as over against "Judaism," has in the context of its own thinking about itself invented an "it" out there against whom, by contrast to whom, it is to be defended and defined. That "it" was the -ism to match the -ity, Judaism corresponding to Christianity. In the context of the Christian component of the historical dialogue with Judaism, therefore, Christianity contributed the naming of the thing, the mode of thought that yielded an -ism as a counterpart to the Christian -ity: namely, Judaism to match Christianity; and Christianity not only named the thing but for its purposes invented that thing, saying what it was and why it mattered.

It goes without saying that over the centuries Christianity,

---

[4]Dunn's excellent proposals (pp. 18ff.), "the four pillars of second Temple Judaism," covering monotheism, election, covenant, and land, seem to me well-justified. My problem is only whether these "pillars" really supported the Judaic systems that will have rested on them; whether they really make much difference in the systemic statements of various Judaisms. My sense is that, while most people will have affirmed what Dunn proposes they affirmed, the systemic statements we have will not have regarded these articles of faith as principal and generative of interesting proposals. To the contrary, these "pillars" are just that: deep in the ground, systemically inert in the systemic writings of various Judaisms.

having invented the category, also defined its contents. This "Judaism" that "Christianity" had superseded was readily defined; and why not, when, after all, it was for the very purpose of self-definition that this other -ism also required fabrication? Accordingly, numerous writers in antiquity knew, when they referred to "Judaism," just what they meant: in practice, circumcision, the Sabbath, dietary laws; in belief, one God, Messiah yet to come, chosen people. While, as I said, we have no reason to doubt most Judaisms will have affirmed all these practices and beliefs, I wonder whether they will have grasped them as the point of cogency, the generative problematic, of their Judaisms. That is to say, while all Judaisms presumably believed in one God and refrained from eating pork, defining those Judaisms in these terms surely misses what was important to the believers of those Judaisms in their Judaisms.

Why Christianity found it urgent to define Judaism for itself hardly presents a mystery. Whether in ancient or medieval or modern times, the issue remained constant and entirely comprehensible; in the language of F. C. Bauer, "how Christianity, instead of remaining a mere form of Judaism . . . asserted itself as a separate, independent principle, broke loose from it, and took its stand as a new enfranchised form of religious thought and life, essentially different from all the national peculiarities of Judaism, is the ultimate, most important point of the primitive history of Christianity."[5]

It goes without saying that the same mode of thought found it possible also to define and set apart and contrast "Petrine and Pauline Christianity," and as time has passed a variety of Christianities have found definition—Gentile Christianity, Hellenistic Christianity, and the like; in all cases, if we know one thing about a system, such as a document, that permits us to classify it in the rubric "Gentile Christianity," then we know much else about that document that the writing itself does not contain. That "much else," then, tells us what is at stake in the intellectual formation of an -ism, in place of other sorts of intellectual formations, such as, for example, "the Torah" or

---

[5]Cited by Dunn, p. 1.

"all Israel . . . except" or "Habakkuk further came and based them on one, as it is said, 'But the righteous shall live by his faith' (Habakkuk 2:4)," which also constitute ample definitions, though hardly for purposes of comparison and contrast.

What Judaism did Christianity invent for itself? The conversation partner fabricated by Christianity hardly presented a worthy opponent for dialogue, or even debate and disputation. On the contrary, once invented, "Judaism" served Christianity as a foil: that alone. Invented for the purpose of polemic and apologetic, "Judaism" was so defined as to form a caricature, a mere anti-Christianity, the opposite, the other, the worst possible choice, by contrast to the best possible choice. So this "it" was "a narrow, legalistic religion. Pharisees taught a religion of 'works-righteousness,' of salvation earned by merit . . . thus providing a stark foil for the gospel of Jesus and of Paul, who, in contrast, brought a religion of forgiveness and grace." Dunn comments in the very next sentence: "The traditional Protestant view of Paul's gospel was derived more from the Lutheran interpretation of Paul than from Paul itself."[6] It would be difficult to show in a more graphic way how critical to the study of the theology of Christianity is the concept of an -ism, in this case, a Judaism: a theological category, defined in theological terms. But the discourse goes awry as soon as we invoke some other category than the theological one to speak of the entire composite of beliefs and practices that characterized all the faithful of (a particular) Israel.

Here is Dunn's language: "A Jesus or Paul who seemed to ignore or deny these characteristic emphases of Judaism they could not understand." Translated into the native categories of the Judaic writings in Hebrew and Aramaic: "A Jesus or Paul who seemed to ignore or deny these characteristic emphases of the Torah they could not understand." The entire frame of reference shifts, the entire argument evaporates; we are now talking about other things in other terms, and the

---

[6]Dunn, p. 14. Dunn rightly points to important Christian protests against this particular "Judaism," naming Moore, Herford, Parkes, and Sanders.

initial formulation, shifted into the native category, loses all coherent meaning.[7] At issue is not merely the defamation of "Judaism" or "Pharisaic Judaism" as "a joyless, narrowly legalistic religion." It is the mode of thinking that yields that whole, that "Judaism," of such a character that, if we know that "it" is present in a part, we know that "it" is present throughout. When Dunn states that "a fresh reassessment of earliest Christianity's relationship with Judaism . . . must be one of our highest priorities," he provides a fine example of the conceptual difficulty at hand; so too his language: "What was the Judaism within which Jesus grew up and from which earliest Christianity emerged? And why did it break away from that Judaism and become distinct and separate?"[8] This is one way of thinking about religion, therefore about the relationships between religions, and it is the way taken by Christian writers from ancient times to the present; hence, in their language, "by Christianity."

Now that we realize how particular to its own mode of thought is the Christian invention of Judaism, we turn to the Judaism that Christianity invented. As I said, in its outlines, that "Judaism" is easy enough to discern, and it is an entirely valid outline: monotheism, Torah, chosenness of Israel, Sabbath, circumcision, pork—whatever. Givens, denominators that serve at the foundations of all Judaisms, these serve as well as any other equally valid entries, or all of them put together; it goes without saying that what characterizes every Judaism can

---

[7]Indeed, when we speak of "Torah" and "Christ" or (as we shall in a later chapter) "Israel" and "Christ," the entire discourse changes in character, and its fixed lines of order and structure blur. If and when a true dialogue gets under way, along lines I shall suggest presently, I should think it will be quite natural to tell the story of Jesus Christ, on the one side, and to tell the story of Israel, God's first love, on the other, abandoning these categories that are not native to Judaism, on the one side, and, I should claim, also not required for Christianity, on the other—Judaism and Christianity, respectively. But we are a long way from that moment at which the category formation will proceed along new lines.

[8]Dunn, p. 14.

have proved systemically urgent to none of them. But what has Christianity made of this -ism that it has invented, what is the Juda- part of the -ism "Juda-ism"? A convenient survey, easy to summarize, comes to us from that great scholar of the history of religions, George Foot Moore.

In his "Christian Writers on Judaism,"[9] Moore identifies the apologetic and the polemic, rather than historical, character of Christian interest in Jewish literature. But apologetics takes the form of dialogue, a Jew and a Christian, because "it enabled the writers to combat Jewish objections as well as to develop their own argument in the way best adapted to their purpose." The Jewish disputant on the Christian side is always "a man of straw, who raises his difficulties and makes objections only to give the Christian opportunity to show how easily they are resolved or refuted, while in the end the Jew is made to admit himself vanquished. This . . . shows that the authors did not write to convert Jews but to deify Christians, possibly also to convince gentiles wavering between the rival propaganda of the synagogue and the church."[10] In medieval times, Christians dealt "not with fictitious opponents, but with real antagonists, who stoutly defended themselves and struck back hard."[11] But, over time, the "dialogue" with "Judaism" took on the character not of an argument to persuade but, rather, of an exercise in vilification. The title of one of these tells the story (Eisenmenger's "Judaism Revealed"): "a thorough and truthful account of the way in which the hardened Jews horribly blaspheme and dishonor the most holy Trinity, Father, Son, and Holy Ghost, defame the holy Mother of Christ, jeer and scoff at the New Testament, the Evangelists and Apostles, the Christian religion, and utterly despise and curse all Christian

---

[9]George Foot Moore, "Christian Writers on Judaism," *Harvard Theological Review* 1922, 14:197–254. See also Haim Hillel Ben Sasson, "Disputations and Polemics," *Encyclopaedia Judaica* (Jerusalem, 1971), 6:100ff.

[10]Moore, p. 198.

[11]Moore, p. 201; in the next chapter we shall see the phenomenon to which Moore alludes.

people." Eisenmenger's Judaism involved "murder of children to use their blood in unholy rites."[12]

Modern writers described "Judaism" as "legalism," "the sum and substance of religion . . . in Jewish apprehension, the only form of religion for all ages." Judaism is then a religion in which "religion is the right behavior of man before God," while Christianity says, "Religion is communion with God; God will admit man to his communion because he is not only holiness but love. In Judaism . . . where his holiness is exclusively emphasized, God remains absolutely exalted above the world and man, separated from them, abiding unchangeable in himself."[13] The Jewish idea of God is "abstract monotheism and abstract transcendentism," an inaccessible God.[14] Moore is straightforward in characterizing this "Judaism" as an invention for the purpose of dialogue with Jews, and dialogue with Jews as a medium for their conversion. When Schmidt told Buber the only basis on which Jews could live in Germany was their conversion to Christianity, he defined the "Judeo-Christian dialogue" in terms entirely authentic to the historic reality. Here is how Moore characterizes Theodor Weber:

> It is equally important to remark that the "fundamental conception" of an inaccessible God, whom, without perceiving the difference, he converts in the next breath into an Absolute God, is derived from the principle that legalism is the essence of religion, from which, according to Weber, it follows by logical necessity. About this he deceives himself; the necessity is purely apologetic. The motive and method of the volume are in fact apologetic throughout; the author, like so many of his predecessors, sets himself to prove the superiority of Christianity to Judaism; . . . it may perhaps without injustice be described more specifically as mission-

---

[12]Moore, p. 214.
[13]Moore, citing Theodor Weber, p. 229.
[14]Moore, p. 230.

ary apologetic: he would convince Jews how much better Christianity is than Judaism.[15]

Weber's influence, to be sure, never matched that of his successor, Emil Schürer, whose *History of the Jewish People in the Times of Jesus Christ* formed the most influential account of Judaism in the German language and, in its English translation, for the larger part of the Christian world.[16]

Schürer's "Judaism" consists of the Law (meaning the Torah) and the Messianic expectation. In his account of "life under the law," Schürer treated the motive for religion as "essentially external, the result was an incredible externalizing of the religious and moral life, the whole of which is drawn down into the juristic sphere."[17] Schürer states, "And all this trivial and perverted zeal professes to be the true and right religion. The more pains men took, the more they believed that they gained the favor of God." Schürer substantiates his picture by showing how heavy a burden the Torah laid on Israel, describing in detail a variety of regulations. Here Moore judges the matter once more as an apologetic: " 'Life under the Law' was conceived not as a chapter in the history of Judaism but as a topic of Christian apologetic; it was written to prove by the highest Jewish authority that the strictures on Judaism in the Gospels and the Pauline Epistles are fully justified."[18]

---

[15]Moore, p. 231. Moore conducts his own dispute with Weber (p. 233): "Weber's antithesis between the transcendent god of Jewish theology and the contrary in Christian theology shows how little he knew about either the history or the content of Christian dogma."

[16]Moore's *Judaism* (Cambridge, 1927) was intended as a systematic refutation, and Jews vastly appreciated the work. But its influence on Christian thinking about Judaism can be described as merely marginal. Judaism would be described from Schürer onward in pretty much the terms Schürer, standing in mid-flood of a great river, set forth. (Subsequent references to Moore refer to "Christian Writers on Judaism" [see n. 9].)

[17]Moore, p. 239.

[18]Moore, p. 240. Moore does not suggest that much of the Lutheran Evangelic attack on "Judaism" served the second purpose of discrediting any other "legalistic" religion, of which the leading candidate must be Roman Catholicism. On the mode of Protestant scholar-

The upshot was that, so far as dialogue with Judaism was concerned, the Christian party found itself well armed for the fray: no dialogue but a war of extermination. Judaism really was no religion at all. Schürer's successor, Wilhelm Bousset, had this to say, in Moore's words:

> The God of Judaism in that age was withdrawn from the world, supramundane, extramundane, transcendent. "The prophetic preaching of the exaltation and uniqueness of Jehovah became the dogma of an abstract, transcendent monotheism." "God is no more in the world, the world no more in God." "What is most completely original and truly creative in the preaching of Jesus comes out most strongly and purely when he proclaims God the heavenly Father." "The later Judaism had neither in name nor in fact the faith of the Father-God; it could not possibly rise to it. And as the whole 'Gesetzesfrömmigkeit' [legal piety] of Judaism is based upon its increasingly transcendent conception of god, so the new conception introduced by Jesus is the ground of a wholly new type of piety."[19]

Moore observes that the sources on the strength of which Bousset describes "Judaism" were documents to which Judaism "never conceded any authority"—namely, apocryphal and pseudepigraphic writings—"while he discredits and largely ignores those which it has always regarded as normative." In so stating, of course, Moore in 1922 pointed toward the work he would bring to successful publication five years later in his *Judaism*.

Moore might well have observed, also, that the caricature framed by this invention of "Judaism" served the Protestant polemic against Roman Catholic Christianity. The invented Judaism presented to humanity

---

ship in religion serving as a medium for anti-Catholic polemic, see now Jonathan Z. Smith, *Divine Drudgery* (Chicago: University of Chicago Press, 1991), who shows that much of the comparative study of Greco-Roman pagan and Christian religions yields a sustained polemic on how the pure faith was corrupted by its Catholicization.

[19]Moore, p. 242.

an arid wasteland of legalistic works-righteousness, with an emphasis on merit and achievement, so that one's good works outweigh the bad works in the final eschatological evaluation of behavior. In short, Judaism was thought to be a religion of scoreboard mathematics. Easy parallels were then drawn between the formalism and bankruptcy of . . . Judaism and similar characterizations of sixteenth-century Christianity, against which Luther . . . reacted.[20]

More than a single purpose was served, therefore, in the invention of Judaism, but among the many, dialogue was not one of them. In fact, if Christians really supposed their Judaic conversation partners were robots of the law, who added up the commandments they did and subtracted their transgressions, so coming up with a salvation via arithmetic, I cannot understand why in the world they would have found such people worthy of dialogue.

We find ourselves confronted with only one possible judgment: there has never been a Judeo-Christian dialogue so far as Christians claimed to be party to a dialogue. From earliest times to the present, Christians have invented a Judaism with which they proposed to conduct not a dialogue but a monologue. So far as people made up dialogues, as Justin with Trypho, or so far as theologians or scholars imagined that they were arguing one side of a debate with a real opponent, we have to classify them as either misguided or hypocritical. Moore's characterization of the entire history of Christian writing on Judaism points toward the latter conclusion: "In all this time no attempt had been made by Christian scholars to present Judaism in the age which concerned them most . . . as a whole and as it was in and for itself. . . . When in the nineteenth century the study of Judaism was in some measure revived, the actuating motive was to find in it the milieu of early Christianity." In this regard the modern period proves capable

---

[20]Bruce W. Longenecker, *Eschatology and the Covenant: A Comparison of 4 Ezra and Romans 1–11* (Sheffield: Journal for the Study of the New Testament Supplement Series 57, 1991), pp. 14–15.

of the greatest inventions; Moore says that "nowhere is a suggestion made that in this respect [abstract monotheism, or a transcendent idea of God as the Absolute] the Jewish idea of God differed from the Christian. So it is also with the 'legalism' which for the last fifty years has become the very definition and the all-sufficient condemnation of Judaism. It is not a topic of the older polemic; indeed, I do not recall a place where it is even mentioned . . . legalism as a system of religion, not to say as the essence of Judaism, no one [before modern times] seems to have discovered."[21]

Why then should Christians have imagined that they conducted a dialogue with Judaism? And, given their sustained and governing concern with the refutation of "Judaism" and the conversion of the Jews, why imagine that what they were writing fell into the category of "dialogue" at all? An early convention, theological apologetics in the form of dialogue, turned out to define an entire genre of writing and mode of thinking about "Judaism." First invented as a category, then given categorical definition, this "Judaism" bore no relationship to any Judaic religious system, its Torah and its piety alike. The Judeo-Christian dialogue on the Christian side aimed from antiquity to its moral disgrace in the person of Karl Ludwig Schmidt in Nazi Germany at only one goal: the conversion of the Jews. So far as Christianity was concerned, "Judaism," once invented, served much as did "Pharisees" for Jesus, as an ever-to-be-humiliated debate partner: the perpetual loser, the example of what not to say, be, or do. Under such conditions, the last thing Christianity wanted was to conduct a dialogue with not its fabricated "Judaism" but "the Torah of Moses, our rabbi," and any comparison or contrast between "Christianity" and "the whole Torah: what is hateful to yourself do not do to your neighbor, all the rest is commentary, now go study"—any such contrast hardly serves an apologetic polemic in behalf of Christianity.

Through time, no one imagined a dialogue between Jesus and Hillel or between Paul and Yohanan ben Zakkai, but there

---

[21]Moore, p. 252.

one can imagine dialogue. In the fabricated category and the invented dialogue, by contrast, the conditions of dialogue are not only not met, they are not even admitted. The Christian party never proposed to take seriously the position of even the "Judaism" it invented; from antiquity to modern times, the Christian party violently denied the integrity of the Judaic; and, it goes without saying, in the figures of Rosenstock-Huessy and Schmidt among many through the centuries, the Christian party most certainly did not propose to accept responsibility for the outcome of discussion. In the first two thousand years of the Judeo-Christian dialogue, Christianity never once contemplated conceding the legitimacy of the other's viewpoint. We shall now see that so far as the Judaic faithful were concerned, there was no conversation partner to begin with: Christianity never happened.

4

The Judeo-Christian Dialogue
as We Know It:
The Judaic Dismissal of Christianity
and the Preferred Judaic Christology

As the third child of three, I understand the frustration of Christianity in its (imagined) confrontation with Judaism: in my memory my brother, eight years older, rarely acknowledged my presence or, more rarely still, my existence. He did when he had to, so it always has seemed to me. The irritation evident in Christian impatience with perfidious Israel therefore is something I can comprehend. In ancient times, while Christian writers from the Evangelists onward addressed the world beyond the faithful, Judaic writers never explicitly conceded the existence of Christianity in the world. So while—in responding to the unpleasant fact that most of Israel, the Jewish people, ignored the new reading of the ancient scripture and the new faith that came out of that reading—Christianity invented a Judaism with whom to conduct disputations or debates (if not what we might call a dialogue), Judaism responded to the unpleasant fact of the advent of Christianity with what was—on the surface—sedulous indifference.

True, veiled references to Jesus may occur hither and yon, such as when sages spoke of Balaam, prophet to the gentiles.[1]

---

[1] See Judith Baskin, *Pharaoh's Counsellors: Job, Jethro, and Balaam in Rabbinic and Patristic Tradition* (Atlanta: Scholars Press, 1983, for Brown Judaic Studies).

And I have argued that important points of emphasis in rabbinic documents brought to closure in the century after the conversion of Constantine responded to significant claims—vis-à-vis the Messiah, the Torah, and the identification of Israel—addressed to Judaism by Christianity.[2] But such allusions—if that is what they are—and so subtle a dispute on critical issues addressing both parties to the debate—if that is what it was—hardly correspond, on the Judaic side, to the articulated and vigorous presentation, to Judaism, of the case set forth for Jesus Christ, whether in the Gospels and the letters of Paul or in the great tractates of Justin, Aphrahat, and the other fathers of the church.

In fact there was a Judaic position on Christianity, and we need not locate it only in the sour portrait of Balaam, on the one side, or in the implicit and merely tacit restatement of Israel's positions on Messiah, Torah, and Israel contained in freestanding documents of the fifth century, on the other. That position consisted of three propositions, one in documents that probably reached closure prior to the conversion of Constantine, the other two in those that came to redaction afterward. The three positions are simply stated. First, Christians pervert the truth because, unlike the pagans, they have the Torah but they corrupt and falsify it. Second, Christians are indeed related to Israel but illegitimately so, the bad seed of Jacob. And third, it goes without saying, Jesus was a man of poor morals.

To the first-century authority Tarfon is attributed the angry observation that there were people around who knew the truth of the Torah but rejected it. So states a saying assigned to him in the Tosefta, a document that reached closure, it would seem, at ca. A.D. 300, long after the first century when Tarfon is supposed to have lived:

The books of the Evangelists and the books of the minim they do not save from the fire [on the Sabbath]. They are

---

[2]Neusner, *Judaism and Christianity in the Age of Constantine: Issues of the Initial Confrontation* (Chicago: University of Chicago Press, 1987); see chapter 2, note 3.

allowed to burn up where they are, they and [even] the references to the Divine Name that are in them . . . .

Said R. Tarfon, "May I bury my sons if such things come into my hands and I do not burn them, and even the references to the Divine Name which are in them. And if someone was running after me, I should escape into the temple of idolatry, but I should not go into their houses of worship. For idolators do not recognize the Divinity in denying him, but these [minim] recognize the Divinity and deny him. About them Scripture states, 'Behind the door and the doorpost you have set your symbol for deserting me, you have uncovered your bed' (Isa. 57:8)."

Tosefta Shabbat 13:5

This statement has long persuaded scholars that the rabbinic authority recognized the difference between pagans and those minim under discussion, reasonably assumed to be Christian. When Christians came under discussion, they appear as a source of exasperation, not as Israel's counterpart and opposite, let alone as ruler of the world and precursor to Israel's final triumph in history.

Second, the Christian empire, Rome, is situated in relationship to Israel, a concession that one gentile nation differs from all the others. Such a concession is possible only within the framework of the Torah, and, as we shall now see, sages concede that Christian Rome relates to Israel in the way in which Israel today relates to ancient Israel: that is, genealogically. In this way the sibling is acknowledged. But when we examine the striking representation of Rome that surfaces in compilations of rabbinic exegesis of scripture brought to closure after the fourth century, we realize the polemic contained within that concession. Rome is represented as Israel's brother—the illegitimate one; as I said, Abraham's or Jacob's bad seed. Rome is identified with Ishmael or Edom or Esau. Rome acknowledged as a relative in a way in which no other nation ever was acknowledged is represented as the one thing standing in the way of Israel's—and the world's—ultimate salvation. So, in the person of Rome, now Christian, Christianity is represented as a ghastly mistake. From the womb, Israel and Rome contended.

1. A. "And all the children struggled together [within her, and she said, 'If it is thus, why do I live?' So she went to inquire of the Lord. And the Lord said to her, 'Two nations are in your womb, and two peoples, born of you, shall be divided; the one shall be stronger than the other, the elder shall serve the younger']" (Gen. 25:22–23):

B. R. Yohanan and R. Simeon b. Laqish:

C. R. Yohanan said, "[Because the word, 'struggle,' contains the letters for the word, 'run,'] this one was killing that one and that one was running to kill this one."

D. R. Simeon b. Laqish: "This one releases the laws given by that one, and that one releases the laws given by this one."

2. A. R. Berekhiah in the name of R. Levi said, "It is so that you should not say it was only after he left his mother's womb that [Esau] contended against [Jacob].

B. "But even while he was yet in his mother's womb, his fist was stretched forth against him: 'The wicked stretch out their fists [so Freedman] from the womb' (Ps. 58:4)."

Genesis Rabbah LXIII:VI

Rome was symbolized, in particular, by the pig, a choice possible only for Christianity; for Christianity exhibits the marks of faith, citing the Torah, but it conceals the marks of apostasy. The pig has cloven hoofs, so it appears to be acceptable. But it does not chew the cud—something not visible to the naked eye—and so conceals its true character. In the next passage Rome appears as a pig, an important choice for symbolization, as we shall see in Leviticus Rabbah as well:

1. A. "When Esau was forty years old, he took to wife Judith the daughter of Beeri the Hittite, and Basemath the daughter of Elon the Hittite; and they made life bitter for Isaac and Rebecca" (Gen. 26:34–35).

B. "The swine out of the wood ravages it, that which moves in the field feeds on it" (Ps. 80:14).

C. R. Phineas and R. Hilqiah in the name of R. Simon: "Among all of the prophets, only two of them spelled out in public [the true character of Rome, represented by the swine], Asaf and Moses.

D. "Asaf: 'The swine out of the wood ravages it.'

E. "Moses: 'And the swine, because he parts the hoof' (Deut. 14:8).

F. "Why does Moses compare Rome to the swine? Just as the swine, when it crouches, puts forth its hoofs as if to say, 'I am clean,' so the wicked kingdom steals and grabs, while pretending to be setting up courts of justice."

Genesis Rabbah LXV:I

Edom—also standing for Rome—furthermore is represented by the fourth and final beast. Rome is related through Esau, as Babylonia, Media, and Greece are not. The fourth beast was seen in a vision separate from the first three. It was worst of all and outweighed the rest. Just as the pig pretends to be a clean beast by showing the cloven hoof, but in fact is an unclean one, so Rome pretends to be just but in fact governs by thuggery. Edom does not pretend to praise God but only blasphemes. It does not exalt the righteous but kills them. These symbols concede nothing to Christian monotheism and biblicism. Of greatest importance, while all the other beasts bring further ones in their wake, the pig does not: "It does not bring another kingdom after it." It will restore the crown to the one who will truly deserve it, Israel. Esau will be judged by Zion, so Obadiah 1:21. The now-Christian empire in no way requires differentiation from its pagan predecessors. Nothing has changed, except matters have gotten worse. Beyond Rome, standing in a straight line with the others, lies the true shift in history, the rule of Israel and the cessation of the dominion of the (pagan) nations.

As to the representation of Jesus in particular, we have the following, which places Jesus in the second century B.C. as the disciple of a sage of that period:

When King Jannai slew our Rabbis, R. Joshua b. Perahyah [supply: and Jesus] fled to Alexandria of Egypt. On the resumption of peace, Simeon b. Shetach sent to him: "From me (Jerusalem), the holy city, to thee, Alexandria of Egypt (my sister). My husband dwelleth within thee and I am desolate."

He arose, went, and found himself in a certain inn, where great honor was shown him. [He said,] "How beautiful is this Acsania!" [The word denotes both inn and innkeeper. R. Joshua used it in the first sense; the answer assumes the second to be meant.]

Thereupon [Jesus] observed, "Rabbi, her eyes are narrow."

"Wretch," he rebuked him, "is this what preoccupies you?"

He sounded four hundred trumpets and excommunicated him. [Jesus] came before him many times pleading, "Receive me!" But he would pay no heed to him.

One day [Joshua] was reciting the Shema, when Jesus came before him. He intended to receive him and made a sign to him. [Jesus] thinking that it was to repel him, went, put up a brick, and worshiped it.

"Repent," said he (R. Joshua) to him.

He replied, "I have thus learned from thee: 'He who sins and causes others to sin is not afforded the means of repentance.' "

And a Master has said, "Jesus the Nazarene practiced magic and led Israel astray."

Babylonian Talmud Sanhedrin 107B, trans. H. Freedman

Judaism's response to Christianity addressed only the figure of Jesus, meaning only to discredit him. So Judaism's dialogue with Christianity in ancient times consisted of (1) the denial implicit in the ubiquitous pretense that Christianity does not exist anyhow; (2) the allusion to people who should know better; (3) the representation of Rome as the fourth monarchy, standing in Israel's way, but only for a brief interval; and (4) the vilification of Jesus. Whether a more worthy dialogue is accomplished by inventing an opponent or pretending there is no opponent but discrediting him anyhow is not a productive issue.

Medieval and modern times brought forth variations on the theme that Christianity never really mattered. Forced to debate under threatening circumstances, Judaic sages in medieval times with great tact but also with surpassing courage formulated issues in an articulate way, facing Christianity and facing it down. This they did by selecting, among available Christologies,[3] the one that served best the interests of hostile polemic: Jesus really was the Messiah, who fulfilled the messianic promises of the Torah.

Christians from Matthew forward insisted that Jesus had kept those promises, and they advanced them with great vigor as the reason for Jews to accept Jesus as the Messiah. A fine example of the character of the Judaic response comes to us from the Barcelona disputation, 1263.[4] The Jewish partner to the dialogue, Moses b. Nahman, tried to persuade the Christian counterpart that the Messiah was not so important to Judaism as Christians maintained.[5] Maccoby states, "If, as Christians thought, the Messiah was divine, then his coming was for every human being the central and essential moment of all history, the moment that counted for every individual's personal salvation." No wonder, then, that, for the purposes of dialogue, Judaism would meet that Christian claim head-on. The condition of the world refutes Christianity, pure and simple: "From the days of Jesus until now, the whole world has been full of violence and plundering."[6]

---

[3]So far as I know, in two thousand years, only one Judaic theologian has ever written in an objective, informed, sympathetic, and constructive way about issues of Christology, Eugene B. Borowitz, *Contemporary Christologies: A Jewish Response* (Ramsey, N.J.: Paulist Press, 1980).

[4]I follow Hyam Maccoby, ed., *Judaism on Trial: Jewish-Christian Disputations in the Middle Ages* (Rutherford, N.J.: Fairleigh Dickinson University Press, 1982), pp. 39–75. Maccoby surveys prior scholarship on this disputation, pp. 57ff. None of the issues concerns us here.

[5]In a different context, I make that same point; see *Judaisms and Their Messiahs in the Beginning of Christianity* (New York: Cambridge University Press, 1987, edited with William Scott Green); and also my *The Foundations of Judaism: Method, Teleology, Doctrine* (Philadelphia: Fortress Press, 1983–5: I-III. II. *Messiah in Context: Israel's History and Destiny in Formative Judaism*. Second printing: Lanham, Md.: University Press of America, 1988; Studies in Judaism series).

[6]Maccoby, p. 52.

The Christian response objected to this material and corporeal reading of matters, as Maccoby sums up:

> Great things wrought by the advent of the Messiah, Jesus, had all occurred not on the crude, visible, political, social level, but in the area of the spirit. In a region beyond human ken, great things had happened: hell had been harrowed. On earth, the possibility of salvation had been opened, and a great institution, the Church, had been founded to develop this possibility, and this institution had clearly been blessed by God.[7]

But, the Judaic participant points out, because of the sin of Adam and Eve, "Cursed is the ground for your sake." If the Messiah has come and remitted sin, how is it that "all this still holds at the present day too; so that in the era of your Messiah, nothing that can actually be observed and sensed has received atonement"?[8] And if the Christian's Messiah has fulfilled the prophetic promises, what is to be said in reply to this?

> The prophet says about the Messiah, "His rule shall be from sea to sea, and from the River until the ends of the earth" (Ps. 72:8). Jesus, however, never had any power, but in his lifetime he was fleeing from his enemies and hiding from them, and in the end he fell into their hands and could not save himself. . . . The prophet says that in the time of the Messiah, "They shall teach no more every man his neighbor, and every man his brother, saying, Know the Lord, for they shall all know me" (Jer. 31:34); also "The earth shall be full of the knowledge of the Lord as the waters cover the sea" (Isa. 11:9); also "They shall beat their swords into plowshares . . . nation shall not lift up sword against nation, neither shall they learn war any more" (Isa. 2:4). Yet from the days of Jesus until now, the whole world has been full of violence and plundering, and the Christians are greater spillers of blood than all the rest of the peoples, and they are

---

[7]Maccoby, pp. 52–53.
[8]Maccoby, p. 118.

also practicers of adultery and incest. And how hard it would be for you, my lord King, and for your knights, if they were not to learn war any more.[9]

Even the title "Messiah" is not particular to Jesus: Cyrus was called messiah (Isa. 45:1); Abraham, Isaac, and Jacob are called messiahs (Ps. 105:15; 1 Chron. 16:22).[10] So the Christian's claim that Jesus is Christ, and that Jesus is unique as Christ, is rejected by appeal to both the facts of the natural world and the dictates of scripture.

The argument unfolded in the Judaic sage's insistence that "the Messiah is not fundamental to our religion."[11] But he further pointed out that, if the Messiah has come, as the Christians allege, then the evidence in the world at hand is hard to discern. Clearly, for the purposes of interfaith dialogue, the issue served well, since it permitted a head-on meeting of two parties to the same issue. But to accommodate the Christian answer, one had already to stand within Christianity, since to neutral outsiders, all the more so to partisan ones, the claim that the prophets' promises had been kept only "in the area of the spirit" formed an implausible response to the misery of the human condition. Scripture promised the Messiah would bring peace, and Jesus had not done this.[12] Beyond that assertion, all the disputes about the meaning of verses of scripture paled into inconsequence: the facts of the world proved the case against Christianity. That is not to say other issues did not figure in the Judaic Christology: for instance, the notion of incarnation, atonement, the trinity, the belief in universal damnation and original sin, and the like. But these conceptions, internal to Christianity itself, dealt with detail; if Jesus was not Christ, what do details matter?

---

[9]Maccoby, pp. 120–121.

[10]Maccoby, p. 125.

[11]Maccoby, p. 119.

[12]David Berger, *The Jewish-Christian Debate in the High Middle Ages: A Critical Edition of the Nizzahon Vetus, with an Introduction, Translation, and Commentary* (Philadelphia: Jewish Publication Society of America, 1979), p. 12.

A considerable literature on "Judaism and Christianity: the differences" in modern times stated the Judaic case for Judaic faithful. Here too a variety of issues emerged, such as free will vs. original sin, sin and atonement, Christian asceticism, faith vs. law, and the like. But at the center, quite properly, stands the claim that Jesus was and is the Messiah. For our example of the modern formulation of the Judaic side to the dialogue to date, among numerous candidates, Trude Weiss-Rosmarin serves as well as any. Her final and climactic chapter addresses the figure of Jesus: "To Christians, save for an insignificantly small group of modernists, Jesus is, first of all, the Son of God and Messiah."[13] But of special interest here, as evidence for that formulation of matters, she cites a statement that proves asymmetrical:

> To us Christians . . . Jesus of Nazareth appears to be absolutely faultless, without spot or blemish, and as such to be the one perfect revelation of the character of God. What God could not do in any book, however good, he was able to do in a living person. . . . When a Christian man is asked about the character of the invisible God, he points out in answer "Jesus of Nazareth," meaning that Jesus shows us what God really is like and loves us to do."[14]

When I claim that the preferred Judaic Christology is Christ Jesus, Messiah and savior of humanity, this somewhat odd and jarring juxtaposition of what is alleged to be said and what is actually said forms striking illustration. Weiss-Rosmarin immediately concedes, "Christianity is predicated on the doctrine of incarnation,"[15] but she immediately underlines the messianic Christology:

> But to Christians, Jesus is not only the incarnation of God but also the Messiah and Redeemer whose future advent is

---

[13]Trude Weiss-Rosmarin, *Judaism and Christianity: The Differences* (New York: Jewish Book Club, 1943), p. 127.

[14]A. Lukyn Williams, *Modern Doctrines of Judaism Considered*, p. 55, cited by Weiss-Rosmarin, pp. 127–128.

[15]Weiss-Rosmarin, p. 128.

announced in the books of the Hebrew Bible. The New Testament is therefore to a very large extent the concerted effort to prove that Jesus was the promised Messiah and that in him all the prophetic promises were fulfilled. Judaism on the other hand maintains that Jesus was not the Messiah, for he did not fulfill the Messianic hopes. . . . not one of the Messianic promises was fulfilled through Jesus. He neither established universal peace and social justice for all of mankind nor did he redeem Israel and raise the Lord's mountain as the top of the mountains.[16]

It would be difficult to find in ancient or medieval writing any more lucid or blunt statement of the preferred Judaic Christology and its polemical power. Jesus is supposed to have been Christ, the Messiah. But the things the Messiah is supposed to do Jesus did not do, either in his lifetime or ever afterward. To Christianity, therefore, the Judaic participant in the dialogue states very simply, It never happened; and if it did happen, it was a lie.

Did Judaism conduct a dialogue with Christianity? In antiquity, denying Christianity existed and at the same time simply deploring the moral character of its founder, in medieval times obligated to debate on Christian terms, and in modern times finding simply absurd and beyond all reason one Christology

---

[16]Weiss-Rosmarin proceeds to a point that, in light of events since 1943, takes on a certain irony: "As far as the Jews are concerned, their own exile and homelessness and the continuation of war, poverty, and injustice are conclusive proof of the fact that the Messiah has not yet arrived, for his coming, according to the prophetic promises, will usher in the redemption of Israel from exile and the redemption of the world from the evils of war, poverty, and injustice" (p. 129). With the advent of the state of Israel, the former of the two conditions can be claimed to have been met, though the hostility of much of Christianity—Roman Catholic and Protestant alike, excluding the Evangelical churches—to the state of Israel suggests that theological considerations of a different order predominate. For numerous anti-Judaic arguments in the ancient, medieval, and modern disputation literature on the Christian side point to the political condition of Israel, the people, without a state, as evidence of God's penalty for Israel's rejection of Christ.

(with all the other Christologies still more ridiculous), Judaism never conducted a dialogue with Christianity; it never wanted to. Preferring to pretend that Christianity never made a difference anyhow, Judaism went its solitary way. So the one side invented a Judaism for the sake of argument, and, to use acutely contemporary jargon, the other side simply "deconstructed" its debate partner, making of Christianity what it chose, which was either nothing or something absurd and beyond all serious consideration. From the very beginning, Judaism did not wish to conduct a dialogue with Christianity simply because, for the purpose of theological apologetics, denial served quite well, thank you; and for the purpose of preserving the faith, a simple and eloquent affirmation of the Torah—joined to the dismissal as absurd of Christianity's reading of the Torah—amply sufficed. The Judaic party never proposed to take seriously the position of Christianity, denying not its integrity but its existence as something to be reckoned with in the setting of the Torah. That is why I maintain, so far as Judaic faithful were concerned, there was no conversation partner to begin with: Christianity never happened.

In point of fact, the entire history of Judaism in Christendom forms an acknowledgment that Christianity did happen and very much mattered. Since in our own day faithful Christians, represented in this context by Moore, Parkes, Sanders, and Dunn among many, have systematically demolished the fabrication of a Judaism as legalistic, a religion of law as against a religion of love, and since the Second Vatican Council in 1965 and counterpart Protestant and Orthodox church councils have affirmed that Israel after the flesh remains covenanted with God, the possibility of a dialogue on the Christian side opens up. For, so long as Christianity in its principal statements adhered to its conception of Judaism and its supersessionist theory of the Torah as nullified by Christ, a fictive Judaism formed the only candidate for conversation with Christianity. Now, because of theologians and scholars alike, an authentic Judaism formed by Christian faithful, from popes and bishops to professors and pastors, stands ready for dialogue. It is fitting and proper, therefore, for me as a practicing Jew to state that the Judaic dismissal of Christianity—it never mattered anyhow, at least to us—in point of fact is simply false.

Indirect allusions to Christian doctrine hardly serve to falsify the notion that Judaism never responded to Christianity and never was affected by it.[17] Nor do I offer in evidence my claim that three of the principal formulations of the Judaism of the dual Torah—its doctrines of the Messiah, the people, Israel, and the dual Torah itself—formed responses to the crisis and challenge of empowered Christianity.[18] The theses of those exercises in academic imagination are only marginally interesting when we consider the claim I offer: that Christianity not only happened but defined the conditions under which, for its part, Judaism also would take shape and take place, from the moment of the political triumph of Christianity in the fourth century to the time of its political disestablishment in the nineteenth. To state matters simply, so long as Christianity governed Christendom, the Judaism of the dual Torah, formed (as I maintain) as a systematic response to the principal statements of Christianity concerning Israel, the Torah, and the Messiah, flourished. At the point at which Christendom gave way to the nation-state and Christianity no longer defined the conditions in which Israel, the people, would endure, then the Judaism of the dual Torah found itself confronted with significant competition from other Judaic systems ("Judaisms"), raising quite other questions than those that Christianity made urgent and that the Judaism of the dual Torah forcefully answered.

In this context, a brief statement of this view of Christianity in relationship to Judaism other than the received one, this claim that Christianity not only made a difference but made all

---

[17]In any event, that was not the intent of my *Judaism and Christianity in the Age of Constantine: Issues of the Initial Confrontation.*

[18]I refer to my trilogy, *The Foundations of Judaism: Method, Teleology, Doctrine* (Philadelphia: Fortress Press, 1983–85), I: *Midrash in Context: Exegesis in Formative Judaism* (second printing: Atlanta: Scholars Press, 1988); II: *Messiah in Context: Israel's History and Destiny in Formative Judaism* (second printing: Lanham, Md.: University Press of America, 1988); III: *Torah: From Scroll to Symbol in Formative Judaism* (second printing: Atlanta: Scholars Press, 1988).

the difference to Judaism in Christendom,[19] is justified. My argument[20] begins with the observation that Judaism as it flourished in the West—that is, the Judaism that found its authoritative statement in the Talmud, its generative symbol in the Torah, and its myth in the story of the revelation by God to Moses of the Torah in two media, oral and written, the oral part now contained in the Talmud—that Judaism was born in the encounter with Christianity in the definition in which it defined the civilization of the West, and that same Judaism lost its power to persuade Jews of its self-evident truth when Christianity did. The birth of the Judaism under discussion here—the Judaism of the dual Torah represented by the Mishnah, Midrash compilations, and Talmud—took place in the year 312, the year of Constantine's vision at the Milvian Bridge of a cross and the words, "By this sign you will conquer." That Judaism ceased to impress nearly all Jews as self-evidently true in the year 1789, with the American Constitution and the French Revolution, which for the first time established in the West a politics distinct from Christianity. With Constantine, Christianity became the definitive power in the politics of the West; with the American Constitution and the French Revolution, Christianity began its journey out of the political arena.

The Judaism that took shape in the fourth century, attested by documents brought to closure in the fifth, responded to that Christianity and flourished in Israel, the Jewish people, so long as the West was Christian. That same Judaism died when the Christian definition of Western civilization entered into competition with other systems of thought. The Judaism that took shape in the fourth century, in response to the political triumph of Christianity in the Roman empire, governed the mind and imagination of Israel in Christendom for the next fifteen hundred years. The reason, I hold, is that that Judaism, for Israel, dealt effectively with the urgent issues deriving from the

---

[19]When the Judeo-Islamic dialogue gets under way, this same matter will require attention in that other context.

[20]See my *Death and Birth of Judaism: The Impact of Christianity, Secularism, and the Holocaust on Jewish Faith* (New York: Basic Books, 1987).

world defined by regnant Christianity. Received for that long epoch as self-evidently true, that same Judaism began to strike some Jews as not at all self-evident, at that point and in those places at which Christianity (in one version or another) lost control of the politics of the West. When Christianity no longer governed the political life and therefore also the symbolic transactions of the West, the Judaism that had taken shape in response to triumphant Christianity and had so long and so successfully sustained the life of Israel, the Jewish people, confronted skeptical questioning among people now standing essentially outside of its system of truths beyond all argument. That is why I say this powerful, effective, important Judaism was born in 312 and died—that is, ceased to form the sole Judaism in most of the world—in 1789: born in the rise of Christianity to empowerment, died in the death of Christianity in its political form, as Christendom.

Why does the fourth century mark so critical an era in the history of Judaism? Because that was when the Judaism that would flourish in the West came to full definition and expression—and so did the Christianity that would define the civilization of the West for fifteen hundred years. The fourth century therefore marked the beginning, in a terrible union of cobra and mongoose, of the two great religious traditions of the West, unequal in numbers but well matched in intellectual resources, Christianity and Judaism. While Christianity took shape around its own issues, the Judaism of the dual Torah responded in a profound way to the challenge of Christianity in its triumphant form. Had a Judaism not done so, no Judaism could have survived the amazing events of that era: conversion of the enemy to the persecuted faith. For Jews had to sort out the issues defined by the triumph of Christianity as well as their own disappointment of the same age. And, through the sages, they succeeded in doing so.

At that time through the fourth and into the fifth century, important Judaic documents, particularly the Talmud of the Land of Israel, were brought to a conclusion: Genesis Rabbah, a systematic expansion of the story of creation in line with Israel's later history, and Leviticus Rabbah, a search for the

laws of history and society undertaken in passages of the book
of Leviticus. These writings undertook to deal with an agenda
defined by the political triumph of Christianity. These questions for Jews? First, the meaning of history; second, the coming of the Messiah; third, the definition of who is Israel. The
triumph of Christianity called all three, for Israel, into question. Christian thinkers for their part reflected on issues presented by the political revolution in the status of Christianity.
Issues of the interpretation of history from creation to the
present, the restatement of the challenge and claim of Christ
the King as Messiah against the continuing expectation of Israel that the Messiah is yet to come, and the definition of who
is Israel—these made their appearance in Judaic and Christian
writings of the day. Issues of Judaism as laid forth in documents redacted in the fourth and early fifth centuries exhibit
remarkable congruence to the contours of the intellectual program presented by Christian thinkers. So in the period at hand,
in political conditions that would persist in the West, Judaic
sages and Christian theologians addressed precisely the same
questions, questions critical to the self-understanding of Israel,
the Jewish people. That fact in my view accounts for the success
of the Judaism at hand—its self-evident truth for Israel, the
Jewish people—in the long centuries in which that Judaic system defined the way of life and the worldview of the Jewish
people: Judaism.

So how exactly did the Judaic system exposed in the later
fourth-century writings deal with the Christian challenge? The
symbolic system of Christianity, with Christ triumphant, with
the cross as the now-regnant symbol, with the canon of Christianity now defined and recognized as authoritative, called
forth from the sages of the Land of Israel a symbolic system
strikingly responsive to the crisis. The Messiah served, for example, to explain the purpose of the Judaic way of life: keep
the rules of the Torah as sages teach them, and the Messiah will
come. So the coming of the Messiah was set as the teleology of
the system of Judaism, as sages defined that system. The symbol
of the Torah expanded to encompass the whole of human existence as the system laid forth the limns of that existence. So the

distinctive Judaic way of life derived, the system taught, from God's will.

What about the importance of the doctrine that when God revealed the Torah to Moses at Sinai it was in two media, written (the Hebrew scriptures) and oral (the teaching of the sages, beginning with the Mishnah)? The canon of Sinai is thereby broadened to take account of the entirety of the sages' teachings, as much as of the written Torah everyone acknowledged as authoritative. So the doctrine of the dual Torah told the Jews that their sages understood God's will, and the others did not. The challenge was met. How so? Jesus, now King-Messiah, is not what the Christians say. God will yet send Israel's Messiah—when Israel does what has to be done to hasten the day. And what Israel must do is keep the faith with the holy way of life taught as Torah—God's revelation—by the sages at hand. The Torah stood as the principal symbol—that and not the cross.

The Judaism that would thrive—that is, the Judaic system of the dual Torah—came to expression in the matrix of Christianity. Before that time, the Christian and Judaic thinkers had not accomplished the feat of framing a single program for debate. Judaic sages had earlier talked about their issues to their audience; Christian theologians had for three centuries pursued their arguments on their distinctive agenda. The former had long pretended the latter did not exist. Afterward the principal intellectual structures of a distinctive Judaism—the definition of the teleology, method, and doctrine of that Judaism—reached definition and ample articulation. Each of these components of the system met head-on and in a fundamental way the challenge of politically regnant Christianity. The Judaic answers to the Christian *défi*, for believing Israel remained valid as a matter of self-evidence so long as Christianity dictated the politics in which the confrontation of Judaism and Christianity would take place. So a Judaism of a particular sort was born in the matrix of Christianity and died with the death of the kind of Christian world into which it had been born, and any fantasy that Christianity made no difference to Judaism has now to be abandoned.

Now, since Christianity made a very profound impact on

Judaism, as much as—all Christian theologians affirm—Judaism on Christianity, the possibility of according a position of equality to the other now emerges. But if there can be a Judeo-Christian dialogue, what principal issues should we place on the agenda for discussion? The second step is dictated by the first. Since we are now able to concede, on the Christian side, that Judaism forms something other than a fabricated debating partner, destined always to lose the argument to its Christian opponent, and, on the Judaic side, that Christianity really did happen and did make a difference, we may now ask each side to tell us what it wishes the other to consider. For so long, monologues juxtaposed by people who really did not want to talk with one another—hence the conspiracy of silence imposed by hypocrisy, the pretense of each side to care what the other had to say—give way to the occasion and possibility for dialogue. What about? Who decides?

Part Two

Two Issues
for an Honest Argument
and
How There
Can Be a Judeo-Christian
Dialogue

5

A Christology and an "Israel" for Dialogue: Jesus Christ God Incarnate or Rabbi Jesus the Reformer? "The People That Dwells Apart" or "Holier Than Thou"?

In the dialogue between Judaism and Christianity, surface chatter covers over profound mutual incomprehension. Neither party addresses what most concerns the other. In my own experience, all that Christians want to know about Judaism is why we "don't believe in Jesus Christ." And, in my observation, what many Judaic participants to the dialogue want to accomplish is an improvement in Christian opinions toward Jews and perhaps even winning Christian support of (or at least diminishing Christian enmity toward) the state of Israel. It is a conversation in which neither party expresses much interest in what interests the other, and in which both parties participate for some purpose entirely irrelevant to the substance of the conversation.

Why should there be a Judeo-Christian dialogue at all? If I may summarize the prevailing theory of the dialogue, it is in two parts. First of all, because both religions appeal to the same scriptures—"the Old Testament," "the written Torah"— we may speak of a Judeo-Christian tradition. If there is a shared tradition, surely there can and should be honest dialogue about it.[1] Second, since Jesus was a Jew, in order to

---

[1]In line with the position of Arthur A. Cohen, *Myth of the Judaeo-Christian Tradition* (New York: Harper & Row, 1969), I argue, in *Jews*

81

understand Christianity, Christians must come to terms with Judaism. Important schools of New Testament studies, aiming to identify those sayings of Jesus that really were said by him, have excluded the sayings that they deem un-Judaic, for example, and still more important circles of New Testament scholarship appeal to Judaic sources as a principal source of hermeneutics.[2] One theological position goes on to distinguish between the Jesus of history, who was born, lived, and died as a Jew, and the Christ of theology. The connection to the dialogue between Judaism and Christianity is then simple.

So the two religions can speak with each other, because Christianity derives from Judaism through the person of Jesus, a historical figure. If, then, we wish to understand Christianity, we peel back the layers of "unauthentic" theology and reach back into the core and heart, the Judaism of Jesus forming authentic Christianity. True, that Judaism may be represented in such a way as to reject the rest of the Judaism of that time or place; Jesus vastly reformed what there was; Christianity then is

---

and Christians: The Myth of a Common Tradition (New York and London: Trinity Press International and SCM Press, 1990), that there is not now and never has been a common Judeo-Christian tradition. But as a rhetorical device, making a place for Jews in the politics of a neutral commonwealth, such speech seems to me entirely honorable; that it also is fictive need not detain us, since much valuable political rhetoric invents what is needed for the occasion.

[2]It is no caricature of much New Testament scholarship to describe the "principle" in these simple terms: "If it's not Greek, and if I can show it's Jewish, then he really said it." The desire to Judaize as much as possible, then, is quite natural. The use of Judaic sources under these circumstances will evince more enthusiasm than learning, and the uncritical appeal to whatever one finds in anything Jewish, from the earliest strata of the Pentateuch to the opinion of the Orthodox Rabbi (thus, the authentic spokesman for not Polish Judaism of about a hundred years ago but the Galilean Judaism of two thousand years ago), solves all exegetical problems. Under these conditions, charlatans thrive and, among them, Jews lecturing to Christians on Judaism in the time of Jesus do very nicely for themselves. I disappointed an audience at Boston University some decades ago, when asked, "Tell me, Professor Neusner, what were things really like in the time of Jesus?" I answered, "I don't know, I wasn't there."

what Judaism ought to have become. For Christians who do not believe in the supernatural Christ, the Incarnate God, an easy faith flows from the notion that Judaism was corrupt and Jesus cleaned it up; Christianity is to be preferred to the inferior Brand X. That apologetic yields a caricature of the Jews and of Judaism, as we shall see. The upshot is a dialogue with Judaism that yields an apologetic for Christianity and a condemnation of Judaism as we know it—not much better than the medieval disputations produced, hardly a model of a genuine interchange of religions attempting to take each other seriously.

Nor has Judaism contributed a more suitable example of how to take seriously another religion in terms of one's own religion. If there is no Christian theology of Judaism, at least some have made the effort, building, for instance, on Paul in Romans 9. But apart from a feeble effort of Rosenzweig to postulate a dual covenant—Christianity for the gentiles, Judaism for holy Israel—no Judaic theology of Christianity has founded a theological tradition of breadth and weight. The "two covenant theory," which we met in its formulation by Buber for purposes of his dialogue with Schmidt, serves the interests of the social order: "Yours is good for you, ours is good for us, so let's live in peace." But no serious theological solution consists in denying now what we, on both sides, have affirmed for so long; we Jews never believed Christianity was a true religion, forming a path to God, for if we did we should not accept gentile converts to Judaism, and Christians cannot believe Judaism forms a valid covenant and at the same time accept Judaic converts to Christianity. The disingenuousness of the Judaic affirmation of the dual covenant is matched by the incredibility of the Christian: after all this time, it was really all about nothing.

In general, the Judaic approach to a theory of Christianity treats that religion within the metaphor of a family, as "the daughter faith," or it regards that religion with condescension ("for the gentiles" indeed!—along with pork and shellfish, I assume), or it deems only the historical Jesus (not the theological Christ) as worthy of serious attention. The apologetic claim of Judaism in its modern and contemporary formulation, moreover, has rested upon the allegation that Judaism sets forth the real, the historical meaning of the scriptures of ancient Israel and Christianity, self-evidently, does not. That is to say, no one can imagine Isaiah really had the Virgin Mary in mind when he spoke of the virgin, or the young woman, who would conceive; or that Isaiah spoke of Jesus Christ when he prophesied about the suffering servant. So, since the prophets did not prophesy about Jesus Christ—such being (so the apologetic in scholarly guise maintains) impossible—Judaism conveys the authentic faith of ancient Israel. The beam in the hermeneutical eye of Judaism, of course, is the Judaic hermeneutic supplied by the Midrash compilations of ancient times, which impart to the scriptures of ancient Israel a rich and contemporary meaning, no more the plain sense of the ancient writers than the Christian one of Matthew.

If, for most of the history of their relationship, Judaism ignored Christianity and Christianity fabricated Judaism for its own use, then no dialogue took place, only juxtaposed monologues by parties agreed they did not wish to accord to each other any form of recognition. In the very recent past, by contrast, a kind of dialogue has gotten under way. Judaism recognized the existence of Christianity—sort of. Christianity conceded that out there, beyond the end of its nose, lurked a Judaism with which to come to terms. But each side adhered to its familiar paths. Judaism recognized Christianity, on the terms of Judaism; Christianity acknowledged Judaism, in a Christian framework. On the one side, Judaism found itself prepared to recognize Jesus as something other than the illegitimate son of a Roman philanderer; later on, in *Toledot Yeshu*, the life of Jesus, Jesus was represented as the illegitimate son of Mary and Joseph, her lover, with a husband, Yohanan, who disowned her.

My grandmother's and mother's *Yoshke Pandra* came right out of *Toledot Yeshu*; the story passed in an unbreakable oral tradition, though my somewhat discreet family never told me exactly who that was or what he had to do with Santa Claus, whose absence from our house was attributed (when I was a little boy) to this same dreadful Yoshke's birthday. I leave it to others' imagination to reconstruct what our Roman Catholic neighbors, on the one side, and Protestant ones, on the other, were hearing at the same time about us. But at any rate, so far as I know, they did not think we made our Passover matzoh with the blood of Christian children; that much we were spared, if not much more: "Christ-killers" for instance, cringing at the Cross, trying to ignore Easter sermons on the radio ("His blood on our head . . . the Jews . . . the Jews . . . the Jews").

But I also have memories of how, with much goodwill, a Roman Catholic neighbor offered me crackers, not cake, on Passover, knowing I wasn't supposed to eat bread; and my entire life and career, aimed at bringing Judaic learning into the mainstream of American culture, forms a tribute to the genuine goodwill of gentiles, especially Christians, who wanted Judaic learning in the very center of things and gave it a warm and engaged welcome. That was so from the beginning, and it is so today: I teach at the University of South Florida, with a Polish Catholic president and a genuinely religious Presbyterian dean and a Southern Baptist chairman, and I write these words in a book published by a press affiliated with the Presbyterian Church.

So Judaism endowed Jesus with a valid pedigree and vocation and even withdrew the profession so many centuries had casually assigned to the Virgin (to speak in Roman Catholic terms for the moment): Mary and Joseph really were married, Jesus was no wanton but a fine teacher, and Christianity conceded that the old Israel endured. How much goodwill poured over wounded souls. But, in truth, neither side gave much to the other or anything of itself. After all, how much do you concede if you finally admit that the other religion's central figure was no bastard but even had something of worth to say? Or if you finally realize that the outsider is not going to go away after all? On these terms, dialogue between equals genuinely interested in the other's viewpoint, conceding even the possibility of learning from the other about matters of shared interest, remains unlikely. For what endures out of the old habitual monologues of mutual malice is an attitude of disdain, on the part of Judaism, and contempt, on the part of Christianity. True, goodwill makes bigots into hypocrites. But as we have already observed, hypocrisy nourishes an already well fed self-righteousness.

Facing a wider world professedly interested in Judaic views, the Judaic theologians found impolitic the retelling of the malicious gossip about the bastard wanton, the bad disciple. Not only so but, for some at least, a reading of the Gospel record yielded more than a few passages worthy of genuine respect: the power of the tale itself, the glory of the moral message—these have always won assent from outsiders to Christian faith. So, quite naturally, in place of the disreputable philanderer, son of a philanderer, Judaic theologians produced the figure they could most admire at least cost: a rabbi. Since, as we shall note, at this very same time Christian theologians pointed to the Jewishness of Jesus—discovering, after so long a spell of inadvertence, that Jesus and his mother, as well as Joseph, John the Baptist, and all the disciples, were Jews—the Judaic Christology (if that is what it can be called) found a sympathetic hearing. Indeed, seeing Jesus in his context required an account of "Jesus and Judaism," and, while more than a mere sage and rabbi, Christianity could certainly concede Jesus was at least that. So, once more, two parties concurred—but without entering into the issue at all.

The Judaic participants to the dual monologue, particularly in modern times, have gladly accorded to Jesus the standing of a Reform rabbi. That allegation derives from one sector of Protestant Christianity, specifically the sector eager to validate the Reformation by insisting that Jesus himself, as distinct from the church that took shape much later on, did not claim to be the Messiah, let alone Son of God, God incarnate, and all the rest. This "historical" Jesus, as distinct from "the Christ of faith," carried forward the Israelite tradition of prophecy. Nothing bars faithful Jews from accepting him, since the bulk of his authentic message, as distinct from what the later church attributed to him, had to do with ethics, love of one another, that kind of thing. Perhaps the most articulate Judaic theology of Jesus derives from Samuel Sandmel, who explained "where

Jews can reasonably stand with respect to Jesus." Of course a view of Jesus "as more than a man" is "uncongenial to Jews, inconsistent with Judaism."[3]

The other view, that "those virtues ascribed to Jesus the man, the 'Jewish Jesus,' are characteristic Jewish virtues, expressed in Judaism and integrally a part of it," yields the Christology of "a good and great man—a prophet, a rabbi, or a patriotic leader—but he was not better or greater . . . than other great Jews." And, Sandmel judges, "These two points probably reflect responsibly the essence of what there is to be said."[4]

What made at all possible a Judaic reading of Jesus was, of course, the separation of "the historical Jesus" from "the Christ of faith." Judaism then could consider the former and ignore the latter. Both Protestant and now Roman Catholic Christianity, in the academy and the seminary at least, do no less. If, after all, as scholarship alleged, the historical Jesus never claimed to have been the Messiah, Judaism could pay its respects and still concede nothing when it praised his teachings. Obviously, the Gospels' allegations that Jesus Christ was crucified on the cross (by the Romans), died, was buried, and in three days rose from the dead to be enthroned on high—these have no bearing on the historical Jesus and may therefore be set aside in the "Christ-of-faith" file, which we (in the dialogue) do not consult. And "the Son-of-Man" sayings could be read to mean merely "man," however Christians understood the phrase. It would go without saying that we can distinguish, moreover, between what Jesus really said and "words attributed to Jesus by the developing Church."[5]

Above all, the Judaic Christology concedes a supernatural representation of Jesus while actually admitting nothing very much, as Sandmel does here:

---

[3]Samuel Sandmel, *We Jews and Jesus* (New York: Oxford University Press, 1965), p. vii.

[4]Ibid.

[5]Sandmel, p. 34.

That Jesus was viewed as the "supernatural" Son of Man falls short of specifying the exact nature of his supernatural being; it was an assertion, not a dictionary definition. Moreover, it was an assertion that was expressed fully within the framework of segments of Judaism and was in no way, in itself, a product of Gentile thinking. . . . Once the followers of Jesus were convinced that he was resurrected, there was nothing inconsistent with their Judaism in conceiving of him as the heavenly Son of Man. . . . Those who did not believe that he was resurrected denied that he was the Son of Man, not so much because they disbelieved in the idea, but because they did not believe in this particular identification.[6]

Had academic theology predominated in Protestant Christianity, the new Judaic Christology formed on Rabbi Jesus—like Sandmel, a Reform rabbi—could have defined a shared agenda for conversation. But both Roman Catholic and Orthodox Christianity, as well as the Christianity of the Protestant pews, as distinct from that of the professors and some learned pastors, worshiped Christ Jesus God Incarnate (not to mention Father, Son, and Holy Spirit) (Matt. 28:19); the body and blood of a reforming rabbi were not offered in the Eucharist.

The trivializing Judaic Christology proved therefore monumentally irrelevant to authentic dialogue between faithful Christians and practicing Jews. And Sandmel stated matters candidly:

We cannot in any honesty dissemble about our opinions. We do not see Jesus in the way that Christians do, and we cannot pretend that we do. . . . [We] do not acknowledge adherence to the traditional Jewish view of the Messiah; therefore it is all the more impossible for us to acquiesce in the Christian views related to or derived from the traditional views. . . . It is not alone that the abstract conception of the Christ is alien to us Jews, but the Christian conception of the significance of the career of the Christ Jesus is equally alien . . . most of us fail to understand even what Christians mean

---

[6]Sandmel, p. 35.

in their use of these terms [sin, atonement, salvation] common to both religions.

Sandmel here points to the critical dilemma of dialogue: an absence of understanding, in our terms, of what Christians mean by their terms, and that is the case whether these are terms we use or do not use. Once we acknowledge that simple fact, we realize that "the historical Jesus" is simply inconsequential when it comes to a dialogue between Judaism and Christianity. Either Judaism addresses Jesus Christ God Incarnate (or equivalently critical formulations of Christian theology) or it fails to address Christianity at all.

The dogma of the Jewishness of Jesus, profoundly important to Judaic theologians in forming a Judaic theology of Christianity—Abraham Geiger's "Pharisaic Jew with Galilean coloring," Heinrich Graetz's praise of Jesus' "efforts to impart greater inner force to the precepts of Judaism . . . his ardor to make the Judeans turn to God with filial love"[7] —served Christian theologians in their effort to define a Christian theology of Judaism. The task of the latter, however, proved both easier and more difficult. On the one side, in an age of virulent racist anti-Semitism, people who confessed that Jesus really was born a Jew were seen to say something quite positive about the Jews, and when, in 1939, "with burning tears," the pope of the time stated, "Spiritually we are all Semites," that statement found ready resonance among Roman Catholics of goodwill toward the Jews. A mere statement of the facts of the Gospels then won some praise as an act of courage; but it was in no way an act of concession. It formed a reciprocal bow to the Judaism that said Jesus was really a fine man after all; and so were, and are, his people. I doubt that anyone saw the fearful symmetry in the juxtaposed monologues: "He really wasn't a bastard"; "He really was one of yours." What the Jews professed, the Christians conceded: a dialogue of vacuities but in context, I suppose, one of great moral courage. But after the murder of most of the Jews in Europe, proceeding uninterrupted by con-

---

[7]Sandmel, pp. 63–64.

siderations of the Jewishness of Jesus, in a different context, that same concession carries slight weight and no moral authority at all.

On the other hand, framing a Christian theology of "Israel" that Judaism could find pertinent proved as parlous a task as defining a Judaic theology of Jesus Christ that Christianity could entertain as not merely impertinent. The reason is that, for the whole of its history, Christianity saw itself as the successor of Judaism, heir of the Hebrew scriptures, now "the Old Testament," the fulfillment of the promises of the Gospels. For one example, the perfect Temple, priest, and offering, Jesus Christ in his death, the perfect atoning sacrifice, ended for all time the Old Testament atonement rite so valued by Judaism. Not only so, but the this-worldly presence of Judaism, in the form of the Jewish people, formed a reproach to the faith; that "his own people" rejected him and still do reject him formed the prevailing Christian theology of Judaism.

The representation of Judaism by Christian scholarship, a polemic against Judaism and an apology for Christianity, carried without a demeaning portrait of the Jews as well. As Solomon Schechter framed matters, "Either the theology of the rabbis must be wrong, its conception of God debasing, its leading motives materialistic and coarse, and its teachers lacking in enthusiasm and spirituality, or the Apostle to the Gentiles is quite unintelligible.[8]

Schechter, of course, did not think that Judaic theology was debasing, its motives materialistic and coarse. But Christian counterparts did, and they said so; and not uncommonly, their judgment of Judaism spilled over into characterizations of "Israel," the people, that rendered implausible the conception of Israel as God's holy people. The theology of Judaism led to pride:

> The two great commandments, love of God and love of
> the neighbor, were of course part of the law [=Torah], but

---

[8]Cited by E. P. Sanders, *Paul and Palestinian Judaism* (Philadelphia: Fortress Press, 1977), p. 6.

even in combination they were not accorded that central and unifying position which they were given in the New Testament. All this naturally led to legalism and scrupulosity, to a belief in the saving value of good works, and the consequent sense of pride which a doctrine of merit inevitably entailed.[9]

Scrupulosity—surely a virtue under ordinary circumstances—joined to pride cannot be seen as a virtue. Judaic scholarship assigned the origins of Rabbinic Judaism (represented by the Mishnah and related exegetical writings, the Hebrew Scriptures as read in the rabbinic Midrash compilations) to the Pharisees; so Matthew Black describes that religion as "sterile . . . codified tradition, regulating every part of life by a halakhah, observing strict apartheid."[10] Sanders persuasively maintains that the standard scholarly view of Judaism (qualified by the adjective "rabbinic") portrayed a religion of "legalist works-righteousness."[11] And this "purely commercial view of righteousness"[12] underscored the prevailing view of Israel: people ready to sell out Jesus Christ for thirty pieces of silver, perfidious robots who practice a legalistic religion.

That this "Judaism" represents a battle in the war, fought now on an intellectual battlefield, of the Protestant Reformation, should not be missed, as Sanders states:

> One must note in particular the projection onto Judaism of the view which Protestants find most objectionable in Roman Catholicism: the existence of a treasury of merits established by works of supererogation. We have here the retrojection of the Protestant-Catholic debate into ancient history, with Judaism taking the role of Catholicism and Christianity the role of Lutheranism.[13]

---

[9]Reginald Fuller, cited by Sanders, p. 51.
[10]Cited in my *Rabbinic Traditions About the Pharisees Before 70* (Leiden, 1971) 33:360.
[11]Sanders, p. 54.
[12]Bruce Longenecker, cited by Sanders, p. 56.
[13]Sanders, p. 58.

And the consequences for the Christian place in the Judeo-Christian dialogue with Judaism are not to be underestimated.[14]

Once Christianity had concluded that Judaism, then and now, was not only false but degraded and demeaning, only a small step remained to reach the conclusion that the "Israel" of the here and now need not be identified with the "Israel" of the patriarchs, prophets, and Christ himself. So while Judaism spoke of holy Israel, God's people, sanctified by the commandments, bearing within its body the eternal life of the Torah—words spoken every time the Torah was read in the synagogue ("who has chosen us from among all peoples by giving us the Torah"; "who has given us the true Torah and so implanted within us eternal life")—Christianity saw an Israel that prac-

---

[14]Sanders redefines matters by insisting that at the heart of Jewish obedience to the Torah is motivation: "rather than seeking to earn salvation by merit points and thereby putting God under obligation to bestow salvation in the final judgment, pious Jews concerned themselves with obeying God's commandments as the means of preserving the covenantal relationship already established by God's initiating mercy upon Israel, his people," so Bruce W. Longenecker, *Eschatology and the Covenant: A Comparison of 4 Ezra and Romans 1–11* (Sheffield: Journal for the Study of the New Testament Supplement Series, 1991), p. 15. Sanders names this "covenantal nomism," meaning observance of the law in a covenantal context. On the one side, the entire structure of Judaic piety, from the circumcision of the male as a mark of the covenant to the tearing of the show fringes of the prayer shawl of the deceased as a mark that he is no longer subject to the commandments, accords with this description and sustains it. On the other hand, the covenantal relationship is permanent, indelible, and eternal, whether or not one keeps the commandments, so describing the keeping of the commandments as a means of "preserving the covenantal relationship" is not accurate. The covenant endures, eternal, whether or not one keeps the commandments, because one is born, physically, into Israel; in focusing upon the law, Sanders simply ignores the doctrine of Israel: the this-worldly party to the covenant. His apology for Judaism, or Pharisaism, accomplishes his goal only by protestantizing Judaism: a covenant proclaimed, with Israel, holy and in and after the flesh, simply bypassed, when, in fact, matters are precisely the opposite: the covenant matters because of Israel and endures in Israel, even in its sinners.

ticed not a religion but a legalism, an Israel full of pride. If (with difficulty) we distinguish between a teaching of contempt for Judaism and a teaching of anti-Semitism, we still find a theological statement that in no way accords to "Israel after the flesh" even a trace of the dignity and sanctity that, in Judaism, "Israel" invokes.

So too in Christianity, Israel is merely "holier than thou," "pharisaical," self-righteous, and arrogant. That is not how Judaism understands Israel and its sanctification. One among many accounts out of the theological writings of Judaism deserves consideration, since it draws a stunning contrast between this prideful, perfidious people and those who were chosen by choosing:

> "In the age to come. the Holy One, blessed be he, will bring a scroll of the Torah and hold it in his bosom and say, 'Let him who has kept himself busy with it come and take his reward.' Then all the gentiles will crowd together: 'All of the nations are gathered together' (Isa. 43:9). The Holy One, blessed be he, will say to them, 'Do not crowd together before me in a mob. But let each nation enter together with its scribes, and let the peoples be gathered together' (Isa. 43:9), and the word 'people' means 'kingdom': 'and one kingdom shall be stronger than the other' (Gen. 25:23)."
>
> "The kingdom of Rome comes in first."
>
> "The Holy One, blessed be he, will say to them, 'How have you defined your chief occupation?'
>
> "They will say before him, 'Lord of the world, a vast number of marketplaces have we set up, a vast number of bathhouses we have made, a vast amount of silver and gold have we accumulated. And all of these things we have done only in behalf of Israel, so that they may define as their chief occupation the study of the Torah.'
>
> "The Holy One, blessed be he, will say to them, 'You complete idiots! Whatever you have done has been for your own convenience. You have set up a vast number of marketplaces to be sure, but that was so as to set up whorehouses in them. The bath-houses were for your own pleasure. Silver

and gold belong to me anyhow: "Mine is the silver and mine is the gold, says the Lord of hosts" (Hag. 2:8). Are there any among you who have been telling of "this," and "this" is only the Torah: "And this is the Torah that Moses set before the children of Israel (Deut. 4:44)." So they will make their exit, humiliated.

"When the kingdom of Rome has made its exit, the kingdom of Persia enters afterward."

"The Holy One, blessed be he, will say to them, 'How have you defined your chief occupation?'

"They will say before him, 'Lord of the world, we have thrown up a vast number of bridges, we have conquered a vast number of towns, we have made a vast number of wars, and all of them we did only for Israel, so that they may define as their chief occupation the study of the Torah.'

"The Holy One, blessed be he, will say to them, 'Whatever you have done has been for your own convenience. You have thrown up a vast number of bridges, to collect tolls, you have conquered a vast number of towns, to collect the corvée, and, as to making a vast number of wars, I am the one who makes wars: "The Lord is a man of war" (Ex. 19:17). Are there any among you who have been telling of "this," and "this" is only the Torah: "And this is the Torah that Moses set before the children of Israel" (Deut. 4:44).' So they will make their exit, humiliated.

"And so it will go with each and every nation."

Babylonian Talmud Abodah Zarah 2A–B

Here is one statement of what "Israel" means to the Israel of the oral Torah; Amos's "only you have I known among all the nations of the world, therefore will I visit on you all your iniquities" (Amos 3:2), "I hate, I despise your feasts, and I take no delight in your solemn assemblies . . . but let justice roll down like waters, and righteousness like an ever-flowing stream" (Amos 5:21, 24)—these form a chapter in the Judaic theology of Israel strikingly neglected by the Christian portrait of a religion that is "holier than thou" and arrogant. Read in the synagogue and studied in the schoolhouse of Judaism, the

Pentateuch, the Prophets, and the Writings all attest to something different from that caricature.

So "Israel" forms a category not of sociology, let alone politics, but of divine theology: soteriology. The world is saved through the Torah, which only Israel accepted (and, in the continuation of the story, carried out; the gentiles could not keep their seven commandments, but Israel made a good-faith effort to keep all six hundred thirteen). Any address to a merely worldly Israel, an Israel after the flesh, which is not at one and the same time also the holy people, sanctified after the flesh and in the flesh (the fleshly mark of the covenant in circumcision was, after all, a considerable issue for Paul!)—such an address is to whom it may concern; it does not concern the real Israel, the Judaism of the Judeo-Christian dialogue.

We identify, therefore, issues for an honest dialogue: matters distorted by Judaism or neglected by Christianity in its address to the other. A dialogue in which the Judaic partner speaks of a merely human Christ, in which the Christian partner dismisses the supernatural Israel after the flesh and also demeans this world's Israel (in our own day, both the people, Israel, throughout their homelands, and the state of Israel and Jewish homeland as well), improves not at all on the matching monologues of earlier centuries.

Then is dialogue possible at all? To a believing Jew, Christianity looks like Judaism yet on closer inspection differs radically, and consequently the Christian family of religions is exceedingly difficult to understand. And while persons of goodwill prefer not to say so, to Christians, Judaism ought to be readily understood, being the religion of "the Old Testament" after all, but in point of fact Judaism as they see it (quite properly, as a matter of fact) is so different from what the Old Testament leads one to expect as to be beyond all comprehension. If Christianity were wholly unlike Judaism, any dialogue with Christianity on the part of Judaism would begin with the recognition that the other is wholly other: beyond all parallels, comparisons, and contrasts. And if Judaism were totally out of relationship to Christianity, any dialogue with Judaism on the part of Christianity would also commence with the understanding that the Christian stood utterly out of relationship with Judaism.

Every Christian knows about Judaism—and what Christians know is wrong. For Christians commonly suppose that Judaism is the religion of the Old Testament, but that is only partly true—therefore wholly false. The root of the difficulty in seeing similarities where there are none, of course, is that both religions appeal to the same writing, which Christianity calls the Old Testament, in contrast to the New Testament, as part of the Bible, and which Judaism calls the written Torah, in contrast to the oral Torah, as part of the one whole Torah given by God at Mount Sinai to Moses, our rabbi. Since we revere as God's word some of the same writings, we take for granted we form a single family. So, we assume, we ought to be able to understand one another. And, it follows, we take for granted that when we speak, we are going to be understood, and when we listen, we are going to understand. But as we have now seen, that is not the case. So what is now to be done?

Theological negotiation—you can have your covenant, if we can keep ours—comes too soon (if it should come at all), when parties to the transaction truly loathe one another. In context, perhaps the only possible answer to Schmidt's "Only as sons of a Germany united through the Christian conception of the Church as the spiritual Israel" was Buber's: "God's gates are open to all. The Christian need not come to them through Judaism. The Jew is not obliged to go to them through Christianity in order to arrive at God." But I wonder whether, in order to reach the end of his affirmation, Buber happily took the road he chose at the outset. A plea for toleration, after all, will have found an even more surly hearing than it did, if it commenced with the honest "God's gates are open to all: through the Torah God has opened the gates." But that is what Judaism, in all its forms, has said to all religions, and Rosenzweig's and Buber's formulation of some other message, however honorable and commendable for the toleration their Judaic theology of Christianity made possible, forms a footnote to a text that has always said, and for practicing Jews surely continues to say, the opposite. To find toleration on grounds of sound social policy, one surely need not purchase a ticket charged against theological authenticity, it seems to me.

Then, if not the dual covenant, what is left? If I accept you only because you are like me ("Rabbi Jesus" indeed), then I really do not like you—for after all, in the end you are not like me but are you. And if you accept me only because your ancestor came from my family ("spiritually we are all Semites"), what acceptance do you accord me when we both realize full well that that ancestor, after all, really did leave home; or, if you prefer, I got out of there ("perfidious Israel" indeed). These reciprocal theories of the other then do more than deny integrity and dignity; they make one wonder why either side cares to enter into dialogue with the other anyhow. What can Christianity learn from these robots of the law? What can Judaism learn from this (mere) rabbi, when it has had, and has, so many prophets, sages, and rabbis to consult? So, framed in theological terms, debating theological propositions, addressing questions of truth and faith, the dialogue comes too soon. For only after a relationship of trust exists can honest argument take place; and dialogue consists in honest argument: debate about the same thing, in the same terms, among people for whom dialogue contains high stakes and yields important religious (as distinct from social or political) consequences.

Start with simple things, then allow matters to take their course—that seems to me the counsel of patience. For honest constructive argument, we do not have to love one another. While some of my best friends are Christians, seeing matters as a whole, confessedly, I do find it difficult to love Christianity: "Love bears all things, believes all things, hopes all things, endures all things" (1 Cor. 13:7)—not just yet. Nor has the hour come to ask Christians to love Judaism, which, as Moore and Sanders among many have argued, they persist in misrepresenting for their own purposes anyhow. But I also do not want Christians, in relationship to me and my religion, to bear a burden of guilt or shame ("It does not rejoice at wrong, but rejoices in the right"). Parceling out guilt is for God to do. There will be plenty to pass around, if God so chooses.

So if we cannot negotiate theological truth except through

dissimulation, and we do not will to desist from the effort to come to terms with one another either, what task lies before? It is to ask questions of not belief but attitude, emotion, and feeling: to ask whether each side may be able to form a sympathy for the other, which today is lacking. What I mean is a sympathy resting not on guilt and regret for a bloody past (on the Christian side) or on resigned recognition of the facts of life and power (on the Judaic side). Such attitudes—shame and guilt, or resignation rich in resentment at what cannot be changed—distort relationships. What I mean is a sympathy flowing from understanding, out of one's own religious resources, of what proves critical to the life of the other.

Can I as a Jew find in the Torah a story that will so shape my imagination as to form in my heart sympathy for Christian belief—making it less absurd ("God in the flesh")? Can my Christian counterpart find in Christ a story that will open the Christian heart and mind to sympathy for Israel on Israel's terms—making it less morally reprehensible ("holier than thou")? I think we can, if we tell, each out of the treasure of our own stories, each one the story of the other. Let me explain how the tale of the Torah may win my sympathy for Christ; the tale of Christ may win the Christian's sympathy for Israel: that much.

6

From Doctrine
to Imagination:
A Different Kind
of Dialogue

We have now met head-on the challenge of making sense of the most deeply held convictions of the other party to the dialogue: the conception of God incarnate in a human being; the conception of the uniqueness and holiness of Israel. For the Judaic faithful, Jesus Christ God Incarnate, utterly unique, and for the Christian faithful, Israel, God's people, utterly unique, present convictions that are exceedingly difficult to grasp. In the disputations of the Middle Ages the Judaic side found little difficulty in dismissing, to its own satisfaction, the notion that a man can be God. The Christian side, for its part, had only to look at the humiliated condition of the Jews to find ample evidence for the notion that the church had superseded Israel. And in modern times the Judaic side did all it could to avoid dealing with the Christology of God incarnate, so as not to have to abort the dialogue at the outset. The mainstream Protestant and Roman Catholic hostility to the state of Israel after 1948, as much as the violent opposition to Zionism before that time, suggests that, as the destruction of the Jews' temple and state in 70 had attested to the sin of Israel and the truth of Christ for Chrysostom or Eusebius, so Zionism and the creation of the state of Israel in modern times form a puzzle to the faithful Christian.

To put matters bluntly, neither side has wanted to say what both sides have had in mind: "What absurdities!" Ordinarily, Christians are too circumspect for such honesty. And when they are not, they embarrass the others. Let me give a single current example. Harvard Divinity School professor John Strugnell, chief editor of the Dead Sea Scrolls, created a furor when he told a reporter for an Israeli newspaper, *Haaretz* (November 9, 1991), that "Judaism is a horrible religion," a Christian heresy, and "the correct answer of Jews to Christianity is to become Christian." That anti-Judaism created a furor, of course, and in his defense Strugnell's friends wrote in a letter to the editor of the *Biblical Archaeology Review* (March/April 1991, p. 15) that he was suffering from emotional problems and alcohol abuse.

But you do not have to have personal problems to allege that Judaism is a dead religion superseded by Christianity, that Jews should become Christians since they have no religion, and similar things. On the contrary, for centuries Christianity has set forth anti-Judaism as standard doctrine. And Strugnell's perfectly rational, if repulsive, evaluation of Judaism as a religion also underlines the difficulty of sorting out the tightly twined strands of anti-Semitism, anti-Israelism, anti-Zionism, Jew-baiting, Jew-hating, and all the rest. How are we to identify the intellectual foundations of this religiously based anti-Semitism broadly believed among devout and learned Christians? I point to three malevolent, broadly held myths about Judaism that have long nurtured anti-Judaism and that now feed anti-Semitism and anti-Zionism among Christians in particular.

First, nearly all Christians view Judaism not as a religion in its own terms but merely as Christianity without Christ, pretty much the same religion but deeply flawed by the rejection of you know who. Judaism is the religion of "the Old Testament," so they suppose, and since, within Christianity, the scriptures of ancient Israel that Judaism knows as the written Torah are to be read in light of "the New Testament," Judaism perverts revelation—and has no Torah of its own. Few grasp that Judaism is not merely "not-Christianity" or that Judaism reads the written Torah in light of the Torah of Sinai, orally formulated and orally transmitted. All some professors of Christianity hear is the twenty centuries' no to Christianity, not the eternal yes to God and the Torah.

Second, many Christians view Judaism as pretty much the same thing as the culture or history of the Jews; dislike of Jews because, not being Christians, they are "different"—or memories of some Jew they did not like—spills over into contempt for Jews and therefore also for Judaism. In its most extreme form, this identification of the ethnic with the religious leads Christians who find Jews "clannish"—meaning that Jews happily form a distinct and distinctive community, as does everybody else—to accuse Judaism of racism. That accusation then exculpates the Jew-hater, just as it was meant to delegitimate the state of Israel in the 1975 UN resolution.

Third, some Christians deny that Judaism is a valid religion which, time and again, has formulated compelling and persuasive answers to the urgent questions facing Israel, the Jewish people, in one crisis after another. Jews find the meaning of their life in the joy of Judaism, and that some Christians do not concede. An ancient enduring people, having resolutely and joyously found the center of its being in its religion ("the Torah") under unremitting Christian and Muslim pressure for many centuries, clearly identifies with a religion of considerable enduring appeal—and this-worldly success.

Dismissing that religion as superseded by Christianity, some Christians find plausible the misrepresentation—also as a dead or merely formal faith—of a way of life aimed at the sanctification of the here and now so as to make possible salvation at the end of time. Worse still, there are Jew-loving apologists, taking over the premises of anti-Semitism, who propose to explain that the rites of Judaism concealed that same "religion of love" that Christians hear themselves preach (but Jews find scarce in practice). So condescending friends defend us by saying that, at heart, we really are Christians after all.

It is too easy, therefore, to dismiss this pathetic town drunk as an aberration. And that explains why we Jews insist that anti-Zionism—holding the state of Israel to a standard that applies to no other on the face of the earth and then dismissing its rights of secure existence among the family of nations, so portraying the state of Israel as illegitimate and racist—really is anti-Semitism. Strugnell presents solid proof that there is no distinguishing among (1) anti-Semitism, (2) anti-Zionism, and (3) anti-Judaism, not to mention the more vulgar Jew-hating, Jew-baiting neo-Nazism. They really are one.

For centuries Christianity has set forth anti-Judaism as standard doctrine. And Strugnell's perfectly traditional Christian evaluation of Judaism as a religion is entirely familiar. He does not differentiate between Israel, the people, and the state of Israel, or between Judaism, the religion, and Israel, people and state. Judaism ought to have disappeared; the state of Israel is racist; Israel the people is exclusivist and hostile to the rest of humanity. Anti-Judaism denies the legitimacy of Judaism as a religion. Anti-Judaism, anti-Zionism, and anti-Semitism concur that Jews and Judaism ought to die; among religious and political programs the Jew-hating one at Auschwitz came close to succeeding in its goals.

Carrying forward a nearly two-thousand-year-old theological position of Christianity, Judaism is further maligned as a religion that ought to have perished at the advent of Christianity. Judaism is moreover to be evaluated by the ("higher") standard of Christianity, with the "religion of love" invidiously contrasted to the "religion of law." Christian anti-Judaism on religious grounds helped pave the road to Auschwitz. The National Council of Churches, speaking for mainstream Protestant Christianity in dealing with concrete issues, rarely has anything good to say about Zionism and the state of Israel. In context, therefore, Strugnell is no aberration. Such attitudes have long been commonplace among Christian Dead Sea Scrolls scholars, because, before 1967, Dead Sea scholarship was conducted mainly in Jordan or under Christian missionary auspices acceptable to Jordan. Strugnell's anti-Judaism is—if commonplace in Christian theological circles—hardly particular to his circle at Harvard. Harvard wants to call Strugnell crazy, but at Harvard he was quite sane for all the years in which he said these same things in private. What was crazy was saying in public what many there say in private.

On the Jewish side, by focusing upon the man Jesus—presenting him, for example, as a Reform rabbi or a marginal Jew or a Galilean pietist (Hasid) or in numerous other this-worldly Christologies—Jews have avoided stating forthrightly what in the Middle Ages, under difficult circumstances, they found the courage to state on pain of death: he was not and is not what the Christians say he was and is. The two-covenant theory that Rosenzweig and Buber put forward forms a massive evasion. Buber may well have told the truth when he stated, "I walk about the cathedral with consummate joy, gazing at it." Then, with much of Christian Germany cheering for National Socialist Germany, the man has to have exercised remarkable powers of incomprehension. Worms, as it happens, has two huge churches, one Protestant, the other Roman Catholic; I too have walked around both, mildly admiring the architecture but full of my own thoughts about what these stones have witnessed. Having read, at the Rashi Museum a half mile away, how the Christians of Worms turned their backs on the Jewish community when in 1934 it celebrated its 900th anniversary of continuous existence, how the townspeople of Worms stood idly by and watched the medieval Rashi synagogue burn down on November 9, 1938, I walked around the massive, ponderous church buildings with a sense of anything but "consummate joy." In such moments, the conception of a dual covenant appears more implausible than merely heretical. And, so it seems to me, when Judaic theology entertains the possibility of a dual covenant, it may propose to say what is politic, but it cannot confess what the Torah sustains and confirms.

So for both parties dialogue has proceeded around the edges of faith, rather than at the center of what truly matters to the other party in the dialogue: "Israel" to Judaism, Christ Jesus the Incarnation of God to much of Christianity. That accounts for the dissimulation and incomprehension that characterizes efforts at concrete dialogue. So, these days, when the Judaic party to the dialogue raises the question of Christian hostility to the state of Israel, the Christian party resists with the observation that these are, after all, political, not religious or theological, questions anyhow; when the Christian party ac-

cedes to talk of the human excellence of Jesus, hearing extravagant praise for what is, to Christianity, of only subordinate
concern, both the Judaic faithful, with its lavish praise of the
man Jesus, and the Christian party, with its patient effort to
accept the praise at face value, carry forward the tradition of
dissimulation, not to say hypocrisy, that has masked the denial
of dialogue for so very long. In such circumstances, it goes
without saying, the Judaic allegation (from the early part of this
century) of two covenants, one for Israel, the other for the rest
of the world (with no special status accorded to Christianity in
relationship to Israel), and the Christian allegation (from the
decades beyond the confrontation with the Holocaust) of two
covenants, one for all humanity, the other for Israel, is simply
premature. How are theological propositions and affirmations
to attain a genuine hearing by people each deaf to the other's
deepest concerns?

It seems to me that only when Christianity can see itself in
the way in which the church fathers saw it, as new and uncon-
tingent, a complete revision of the history of humanity from
Adam onward, not a subordinate and heir of Judaism, and
when Judaism can see itself in the way in which the sages of the
oral Torah saw it, as the statement of God's Torah for all humanity, that the two religions will recognize this simple fact:
they really are totally alien to one another. Then, and only
then, does a genuine and an honest meeting with the other
commence. Dialogue will begin with the recognition of difference, with a search for grounds for some form of communica-
tion, rather than with the assumption of sameness and the
search for commonalities. People wish to read the Gospels, in
particular, in the context of Judaism and the sources of Judaism of that time and place. But much that the Gospel narrative
takes for granted proves surprising to a Jewish reader.

Then how do I propose to proceed from this ground zero
that I claim forms our common location? Let me begin the
work of defining a new foundation for dialogue by making one
point only. It is that the only way for a Judaic believer to understand Christianity is *within Judaic terms,* and the only way for a
Christian believer to understand Judaism is *within Christian*

terms. Let me state matters negatively. If, out of the resources of Judaism, I cannot take Christianity so seriously as to wish to conduct a dialogue, then I cannot honestly claim to argue, to enter into honest exchange. If to conduct a dialogue with Judaism, in particular, Christianity has to deny what it has claimed for two thousand years, then the Christian party condescends or dissimulates. And if out of shame for the Christian contribution to the Holocaust (and all the holocausts before this one) Christianity denies its own long-held truth, what good can come of dialogue? And how, out in the parishes, will the priests explain to the people that what they have long believed about Judaism is really wrong—together with the Christian faith that sustained these beliefs about the other? The purpose of dialogue is neither to convert the Jews to Christianity nor to persuade the Christians to give up Christianity in sheer disgust: the two are equally improper aspirations.

Since Judaism and Christianity form quite different religions with little in common, it is time for each religion to try to make sense of the other—but to make sense of the stranger wholly in one's own terms. Can I, as a Jew and a believer in Judaism, understand in my context, in my terms of faith, the religion of the Christian? Can I frame a Judaic religious understanding of the religion of Christianity? What it means to understand another religion demands a definition. Up to now, as I already have noted, some rather unsuccessful efforts at theologies, each of the other, have shown us what not to attempt: a Christian theology of Judaism proves, if not condescending, then un-Christian, conceding more than Christianity has ever conceded in the past; and a Judaic theology of Christianity gives no less—and no more authentically. Judaism cannot concede that Jesus Christ is what the Christians say, and any other judgment upon Jesus Christ is simply beside the point. Christianity may concede that we retain our covenanted relationship with God, but it cannot then admit that converts to Judaism have taken the right route to salvation. So all that Christianity concedes is that Judaism is all right for the Jews, a concession to be sure, but not of vast consequence. But if not a theological understanding of each other, what other understanding can we seek?

My answer commences with a necessary recognition: the commonplace fact that, after all, we really do worship one God, who is the same God, and who is the only God; we and the Muslims with us. So dialogue is required among the three faiths that claim to worship one and the same God, the only God. Within that common ground of being, a human task emerges before us. It is to seek in the religious experience of the other, the stranger and outsider, that with which we, within our own world, can identify. I cannot ask the Christian to deny Jesus Christ as Incarnate God, and I also cannot ask myself to believe that Jesus Christ was and is God Incarnate. But I must try to understand how I can understand the incarnation of God: precisely what is the other side saying? If I am able to locate, in my religious resources, something that will help me to grasp what, within the other's religious resources, the other party is saying, then the other, while remaining other and different, no longer stands beyond the range of understanding. To begin with, can I sympathize: that is, feel how the other feels, the other remaining other? The answer is, Yes, I can, if I find in my own world analogies that permit me in some measure to feel and so understand what the other feels and affirms in the world of that other. So the critical challenge as the two extraordinarily complex and diverse religions seek to communicate begins not with the negotiation of theological difference, with its intellectual tasks, but with the pathos of alien feeling: can I, in my life, feel what the other feels in the other's life?

In simple words, when I can say, "Yes, I know how you feel," I begin to be able to enter into the realm of feeling, thence attitude, thence even thought, of that "you." But so long as I do not know how the other feels, I will listen in sheer incredulity to the attitudes and thoughts of that other. And while diverse cultures nurture different attitudes, and various religions, different theologies, joy or sorrow or love or hope or despair—with these feelings, and the experiences that provoke them, God has endowed us all. When, therefore, I know how the other feels because I have felt the same way, then I may talk with the other, even about other things.

What moves me, as distinct from what persuades me, is the

story the other person tells. Then I can identify with someone in the story or with the storyteller; then, in the present context, I can find among my stories a story that matches the story of the other. To take a homely example, when I had read, particularly in the Gospel of John, how Jesus tries to prepare his disciples for the lives they are going to lead, how he warns them but also strengthens them, I found it easy, as a person who has undertaken to educate young people to change the world, to identify with Jesus: his message, his disciples, and their situation. Here was no doctrine, only an implicit story, and how readily did that story make sense to me, not because it was my story (I never sent out my students as apostles), but because in my story I could find resonance in his story: the pain, the anguish.

In more objective circumstances, how are we to do this? I mean, how are we to find a story of our own that will open us to the story of the other? For that is what I conceive to be the way, until now not much trodden, to communicate, faith to faith. To answer the question, let me give a single example of what it will take, then generalize; in the chapters beyond, I shall then attempt to carry out what I propose here.

My example involves the Virgin, because that is a figure critical to Roman Catholic Christianity and exceedingly difficult for a Judaic believer to understand in Judaic terms.[1] Because of growing up in Roman Catholic New England, living in a Protestant suburb with an Irish- and Italian-Catholic minority excluded, as were we Jews, from the commonwealth of our peers, I take Roman Catholic Christianity as seriously as Protestant Christianity and try to understand its distinctive faith. So I choose as my example a belief distinctive to Roman Catholicism and assuredly as alien to Judaism as the conception of

---

[1] I presented this argument in 1990 in lectures under the auspices of the Roman Catholic community of service, the Community of St. Giles (Communità di S. Egidio/Gemeinde des S. Egidius/Communidad de San Egidio), in Genoa, Novara, Rome, Naples, and Bari and found a sympathetic hearing among clergy and lay members alike, so I am confident Roman Catholics will find the proposal not offensive and, perhaps, one of genuine sympathy.

Jesus Christ the Incarnation of God. The notion of a woman
with a special claim on God's attention—how am I as a Jew to
grasp this? By "as a Jew," I mean, out of the resources of
Judaism how am I to make sense of something so absurd as the
notion that God has a mother? If, after all, I cannot swallow the
gnat, the conception of God incarnate in a man, shall I not
choke on the fishbone, God's mother?

The answer is by finding in my own tradition an analogy that
will tell me what, in my context, Mary stands for in her context.
How can I feel, in my world, the way in which Roman Catholics
(not to mention Orthodox Christians) feel in their world when
they address their prayers to the Virgin? Jews have trouble
enough dealing with Jesus in the Christian reading not of his
life and teachings, with which we can identify, but the claim
that in a unique way he is God's only begotten son. What then
are we to make of Mary? Mary, after all, called "Mother of
God" and revered and loved by Roman Catholics, is bearer of
profound religious sentiments indeed. But if we cannot grasp
how any one man is more God's son than any other, how can
we make sense of how any one woman is more God's mother
than any other? That is why, in the serious exchange of belief
and conviction that, in our own time, Roman Catholics and
Jews undertake, we bypass Mary in silence. In the Judeo-
Christian dialogue with Roman Catholic Christianity, we have
known by tradition how to deal. We dissimulate, with smiles
and good cheer. Just as, in the contemporary dialogue, most of
us bypass Christology altogether[2] —settling for "He was a
great man, oh, was he a great man! How I love that great
Galilean rabbi!"—so of course we pretend Catholics are Protestants, for whom Mary is not a critical figure, and in the dialogue with Roman Catholics we deny by our silence the Roman
Catholic reverence for Mary and worship through her of the
God we share with them.

To make my point about listening to the other's story and
finding among my stories a tale that tells me what the other
feels in the other's story, I have first to call attention to Mat-

---

[2]The exception is Eugene Borowitz, cited in chapter 4, note 3.

thew's representation of the flight into Egypt, because it will show that what I shall present as a Judaic equivalent to Mary's relationship to God is specific and particular, not general and abstract:

> . . . and going into the house they saw the child with Mary his mother, and they fell down and worshiped him. . . .
>
> . . . an angel of the Lord appeared to Joseph in a dream and said, "Rise, take the child and his mother, and flee to Egypt. . . . " And he rose and took the child and his mother by night, and departed to Egypt. . . .
>
> Then Herod, when he saw that he had been tricked by the wise men, was in a furious rage, and he sent and killed all the male children in Bethlehem and in all that region who were two years old or under. . . . Then was fulfilled what was spoken by the prophet Jeremiah:
>
> > "A voice was heard in Ramah,
> > wailing and loud lamentation,
> > Rachel weeping for her children;
> > she refused to be consoled,
> > because they were no more."
>
> But when Herod died, behold, an angel of the Lord appeared in a dream to Joseph in Egypt, saying, "Rise, take the child and his mother, and go to the land of Israel, for those who sought the child's life are dead."
>
> And he rose and took the child and his mother, and went to the land of Israel.
>
> Matthew 2:11, 13–14, 16–21

What is important here is that Mary is represented as a figure much like Rachel, protecting her children and weeping for them. The flight to Egypt in the story of Jesus is represented as a counterpart to the exile of Israel in the time of Jeremiah. Jesus stands for Jeremiah, Mary for Rachel, in Matthew's account.

Do I have a story to tell too? In fact, I have found a figure in the Judaic reading of the Torah that stands in Judaism for some of the things that, in Roman Catholic Christianity, Mary represents. And because of that story, in a direct and parallel way, I can feel some of the feelings that this story in Matthew elicits: the sadness of the mother's love, the providential protection of the mother. So the capacity of Roman Catholic Christians to revere Mary, the power of Mary to arouse in Catholic hearts and souls a greater love for God than they would otherwise feel—the response to Mary and the power of Mary seem not so alien as they did before. For what Mary stands for is a woman who bears a special—a unique—relationship to God, a relationship so compelling that God will respond to Mary in a way in which God will not respond to any other person. So when I ask myself, Do we have, in the Judaic reading of scripture, a figure that can show me how a woman may accomplish with God what no man can do? I of course find the answer ready at hand.

Once I have asked the question in that way—Do we have in Judaism a counterpart to Mary, a live and lovely woman to whom God listens, whose prayers carry weight more than any man's?—the answer is self-evident. And, curiously, the Judaic Mary plays a critical role in the very passage in which Mary and Jesus figure as principals. The story of the birth of Jesus to the Virgin Mary draws attention to the one figure in the Hebrew Scriptures that provides a counterpart; not only so, but the very way in which Mary's ancient Israelite counterpart enters the tale is exactly the way in which, in the ancient sages' reading of scripture, Rachel plays her part. Mary in the Gospel of Matthew flees with Joseph and the infant Jesus into exile. As she goes into exile, so the first Gospel indicates, there is weeping for the slaughter of the infant children, and the one who weeps is Rachel.

Now to the Judaic reader, the story of exile, slaughter, and mourning involving Rachel is strikingly familiar. For we find in the rabbinic reading of the book of Lamentation, in the work Lamentations Rabbah, a closely parallel account. Indeed, the intervention of Rachel in the story at hand runs so close to the Roman Catholic conception of the Virgin's power to intervene and intercede that, understanding and feeling the anguish of Rachel, I can reach out also to the Roman Catholic capacity to invoke the power of Mary, virgin and saint, in her special relationship to God.

Lest these statements seem extravagant, let me forthwith lay out the representation of Rachel and her special power before God. What is important to me in this presentation is not merely that Rachel weeps for Israel going into exile the way Rachel weeps, in the First Gospel, for the slaughter of the innocents as Joseph, Mary, and Jesus go into exile. That parallel is interesting and illuminating but not to the point. What I find striking is the parallel between Rachel's unique relationship to God and Mary's unique relationship to God. For that is something we Jews are not accustomed to noting, and yet here it is.

R. Samuel bar Nahmani said, "[When God contemplated destroying the Temple and sending the Israelites in Exile to Babylon,] Abraham forthwith commenced speaking before the Holy One, blessed be he, saying to him, 'Lord of the world, when I was a hundred years old, you gave me a son. And when he had already reached the age of volition, a boy thirty-seven years of age, you told me, "Offer him up as a burnt-offering before me"!

" 'And I turned mean to him and had no mercy for him, but I myself tied him up. Are you not going to remember this and have mercy on my children?'

"Isaac forthwith commenced speaking before the Holy One, blessed be he, saying to him, 'Lord of the world, when father said to me, "God will see to the lamb for the offering for himself, my son" (Gen. 22:8), I did not object to what you had said, but I was bound willingly, with all my heart, on the altar, and spread forth my neck under the knife. Are you not going to remember this and have mercy on my children!'

"Jacob forthwith commenced speaking before the Holy One, blessed be he, saying to him, 'Lord of the world, did I not remain in the house of Laban for twenty years? And when I went forth from his house, the wicked Esau met me and wanted to kill my children, and I gave myself over to death in their behalf. Now my children are handed over to their enemies like sheep for slaughter, after I raised them like fledglings of chickens. I bore on their account the anguish of raising children, for through most of my life I was pained greatly on their account. And now are you not going to remember this and have mercy on my children?'

"Moses forthwith commenced speaking before the Holy One, blessed be he, saying to him, 'Lord of the world, was I not a faithful shepherd for the Israelites for forty years? I ran before them in the desert like a horse. And when the time came for them to enter the land, you issued a decree against me in the wilderness that there my bones would fall. And now that they have gone into exile, you have sent to me to mourn and weep for them.'

"Then Moses said to Jeremiah, 'Go before me, so I may go and bring them in and see who will lay a hand on them.'

"Said to him Jeremiah, 'It isn't even possible to go along the road, because of the corpses.'

"He said to him, 'Nonetheless.'

"Forthwith Moses went along, with Jeremiah leading the way, until they came to the waters of Babylon.

"They saw Moses and said to one another, 'Here comes the son of Amram from his grave to redeem us from the hand of our oppressors.'

"An echo went forth and said, 'It is a decree from before me.'

"Then said Moses to them, 'My children, to bring you back is not possible, for the decree has already been issued. But the Omnipresent will bring you back quickly.' Then he left them.

"Then they raised up their voices in weeping until the sound rose on high: 'By the rivers of Babylon there we sat down, yes, we wept' (Ps. 137:1).

"When Moses got back to the fathers of the world, they said to him, 'What have the enemies done to our children?'

"He said to them, 'Some of them he killed, the hands of some of them he bound behind their back, some of them he put in iron chains, some of them he stripped naked, some of them died on the way, and their corpses were left for the vultures of heaven and the hyenas of the earth, some of them were left for the sun, starving and thirsting.'

"Then they began to weep and sing dirges: 'Woe for what has happened to our children! How have you become orphans without a father! How have you had to sleep in the hot sun during the summer without clothes and covers! How have you had to walk over rocks and stones without shoes and sandals! How were you burdened with heavy bundles of sand! How were your hands bound behind your backs! How were you left unable even to swallow the spit in your mouths!'

"Moses then said, 'Cursed are you, O sun! Why did you not grow dark when the enemy went into the house of the sanctuary?'

"The sun answered him, 'By your life, Moses, faithful shepherd! They would not let me nor did they leave me alone, but beat me with sixty whips of fire, saying, "Go, pour out your light." '

"Moses then said, 'Woe for your brilliance, O temple, how has it become darkened! Woe that its time has come to be destroyed, for the building to be reduced to ruins, for the school children to be killed, for their parents to go into captivity and exile and the sword!'

"Moses then said, 'O you who have taken the captives! I impose an oath on you by your lives! If you kill, do not kill with a cruel form of death, do not exterminate them utterly, do not kill a son before his father, a daughter before her mother, for the time will come for the Lord of heaven to exact a full reckoning from you!'

"The wicked Chaldeans did not do things this way, but they brought a son before his mother and said to the father, 'Go, kill him!' The mother wept, her tears flowing over him, and the father hung his head.

"And further Moses said before him, 'Lord of the world! You have written in your Torah, "Whether it is a cow or a ewe, you shall not kill it and its young both in one day" (Lev. 22:28).

" 'But have they not killed any number of children along with their mothers, and yet you remain silent!'

"Then Rachel, our mother, leapt to the fray and said to the Holy One, blessed be he, 'Lord of the world! It is perfectly self-evident to you that your servant, Jacob, loved me with a mighty love, and worked for me for father for seven years, but when those seven years were fulfilled, and the time came for my wedding to my husband, father planned to substitute my sister for me in the marriage to my husband.

" 'Now that matter was very hard for me, for I knew the deceit, and I told my husband and gave him a sign by which he would know the difference between me and my sister, so that my father would not be able to trade me off. But then I regretted it and I bore my passion, and I had mercy for my sister, that she should not be shamed. So in the evening for my husband they substituted my sister for me, and I gave my sister all the signs that I had given to my husband, so that he would think that she was Rachel.

" 'And not only so, but I crawled under the bed on which he was lying with my sister, while she remained silent, and I made all the replies so that he would not discern the voice of my sister.

" 'I paid my sister only kindness, and I was not jealous of her, and I did not allow her to be shamed, and I am a mere mortal, dust and ashes. Now I had no envy of my rival, and I did not place her at risk for shame and humiliation.

" 'But you are the King, living and enduring and merciful. How come then you are jealous of idolatry, which is nothing, and so have sent my children into exile, allowed them to be killed by the sword, permitted the enemy to do whatever they wanted to them?'

"Forthwith the mercy of the Holy One, blessed be he, welled up, and he said, 'For Rachel I am going to bring the Israelites back to their land.'

"That is in line with this verse of Scripture: 'Thus said the Lord: A cry is heard in Ramah, wailing, bitter weeping, Rachel weeping for her children. She refuses to be comforted for her children, who are gone. Thus said the Lord, Restrain your voice from weeping, your eyes from shedding tears; for there is a reward for your labor, declares the Lord; they shall return from the enemy's land, and there is hope for your future, declares the Lord: your children shall return to their country' " (Jer. 31:15–17)."

What I find striking in this story is how very much Rachel is like Mary (or Mary like Rachel): that is, the one who succeeds when all other intervention fails. Abraham, Isaac, Jacob, and Moses—the four most important figures in the firmament of Judaism—all make appeals that God forgive the Israelites, who had sinned, and not take them into exile and destroy their holy city and temple. Nothing much happens. The holy men are told by an implacable God, "It is a decree from before me." All the people can hope for is that, in due course, when the sin is expiated by suffering, God will be reconciled with them and restore them to the land.

Moses has to report this back to "the fathers of the world," Abraham, Isaac, and Jacob. The dirge then rises, curses of nature's witnesses to Israel's catastrophe. And this yields the climax: "And yet you remain silent": namely, God. Rachel speaks in the same manner as the fathers of the world, Abraham, Isaac, and Jacob. But she speaks not of sacrifice but of love, invoking her power of expressing love for her sister through self-restraint and self-sacrifice. This address of Rachel's introduces into the argument with God what the men had not invoked, which is the relationships within the family. Rachel's message to God is to relate to Israel the love that comes from within the family, the holy family. Let God love Israel as much as Rachel had loved Leah. Should Rachel not have been jealous? She should have been. Did she not have the right to demand justice for herself? She did. Yet look at Rachel. And, Rachel's message goes on to God: If I could do it, so can you. Why this excess of jealousy for idolatry, which is nothing, that "you have sent my children into exile?" And God responds not to Abraham, Isaac, Jacob, Moses, or Jeremiah but to Rachel: "For Rachel I am going to bring the Israelites back to their land." And he did. "Stop crying, Rachel, enough already; your children shall return to their country." So too as Joseph, Mary, and Jesus go into exile, Rachel weeps, and the result is the same: the family will come home and does come home.

That's why I can find in Mary a Roman Catholic Christian Rachel, whose prayers count when the prayers of great men, fathers of the world, fall to the ground. God listens to the mother, God responds to her plea, because—so Hosea has it, among so many of the prophets—God's love for us finds its analogy and counterpart in the love of the husband for the wife and the wife for the husband and the mother for the children, above all, that love. No wonder when Rachel weeps, God listens. How hard, then, can it be for me to find in Mary that sympathetic special friend that Roman Catholics have known for two thousand years? Not hard at all. So yes, if Rachel, why not Mary? But then, as I have become fluent in Catholic (and speak pretty decent Protestant too), that now seems to me self-evident.

Is this just a scholastic point about parallels? At stake, in fact, is not an argument about parallels at all; my point is just the opposite. My problem with Mary, the heart of Roman Catholic Christianity, is how to find a way of understanding, with empathy, what Roman Catholics say about her and, more to the point, how they feel. If the Roman Catholic faith centers, as it does, upon a figure that is wholly other, with whom I cannot identify, for whom, in my own experience, I can find no counterpart, then in the end I can never make sense of the things Roman Catholic Christians cherish. But if I can say, Yes, in your world your path leads you to the feet of Mary, and coming out of my world I can follow that quest and that yearning of yours, then there can be sympathy, perhaps even empathy.

The importance of Rachel for me, in this context, is that in her I can find that counterpart and model of the woman who has God's ear. Then Roman Catholic Christianity in its reverence for the Virgin faith is no longer wholly other. It is not my own, never was, never can be. But it is a faith I can grasp, try to understand, learn to perceive with respect as a road to God, to the same God who gave me the Torah at Sinai and to whom I said, at Sinai, in Israel, the holy people: "We shall do and we shall obey." That God, who demands obedience, hears the voice of Rachel, so why not Mary? The two religions are utterly different, bearing different messages and distinctive meanings, each for its own faithful. And they remain utterly different. But to me, Roman Catholic reverence for Mary no longer seems absurd or "superstitious" or "insane" or any of the other things we say and think when we simply do not comprehend the other. For out of my religion I can make sense of that other, that different religion. I can find something that makes sense to me to make sense, also, of the wholly other: I can feel toward Rachel something of what, I believe, my Roman Catholic colleague feels toward Mary. And that—as I shall explain at the end—seems to me to define the task for the coming century, in which, for the first time in two millennia, goodwill joins Christians and Jews in the service of the One God—whom alone we now serve—for the first time ever, together.

Why the medium of a tale, my tale, to help me understand a tale, the other's tale? First, because stories touch the heart; they are immediate, direct, unmediated. Second, because stories that touch the heart elicit sympathy; I can feel for the other, reach out beyond myself. The anguish of the mother as a father I can know; the reproach of the mother directed toward the father as a son I can appreciate. And this takes place not in the framework of this world and the family but in the heights of heaven, with Rachel weeping and rebuking God, because she has every right to be listened to by God: you owe, I gave, at least a hearing. And that is all, after all, that Roman Catholics ever ask Mary to get for them: a hearing from the Son (who, we shall see, here and now was and is God Incarnate). As a father and a son I understand, but that is beside the point of Judeo-Christian dialogue. As a faithful Jew studying the Torah I understand, which makes possible the effort to understand the other that, at the difficult and tentative first steps of Judeo-Christian dialogue, we hope to realize.

Now to return to the question: Can I as a Jew tell a tale out of the Torah to help me understand the Christian's tale about

how God walked on earth, how in Jesus Christ, in the words of
Lukyn Williams, "When a Christian man is asked about the
character of the invisible God, he points out in answer 'Jesus of
Nazareth,' meaning that Jesus shows us what God really is like
and loves us to do"?[3] And can I point out to Christians stories
they tell that will help them understand my tale of who and
what is Israel? In hearing my stories, I shall understand the
feeling of the Christian, and in hearing the Christian's stories,
the Christian will understand the feeling of the Jew, when
Christ as God Incarnate, and Israel as the unique and holy
people, meet one another in our shared dialogue about what
truly counts to each—and genuinely puzzles the other. First,
are there Judaic resources that nourish sympathy for the Christian response to Christ, God with us? Yes there are, and let me
tell you some Jewish stories.

---

[3]Cited from Weiss-Rosmarin, above.

Part Three

Undertaking
Dialogue

7

A Judaic Telling
of the Christian Tale
of Jesus Christ
God Incarnate:
Judaic Resources
for Imagining Christ

A subdivision of anthropomorphism, the incarnation of God in general entails the representation of God as consubstantial with the human person in, first, corporeal form, second, traits of emotions and other virtues, and, third, action. God is represented in incarnate form when God looks like a human being (ordinarily, in the case of Judaism, a man), exhibits virtues and expresses emotions like those of mortals, and does concrete deeds in a corporeal manner, pretty much as do human beings. The representation of God incarnate will not have surprised the authors of a variety of Judaic documents, beginning with the compilers of the Pentateuch, beginning with Genesis 1:9: "Let us make man in our image and likeness." Some speaking explicitly, others in subtle allusions, prophets and apocalyptic writers, exegetes and sages, mystics and legists, all maintained that notion.

Here is how Genesis 1:9 is read so as to give explicit notion to the conception of the incarnation of God:

1. A. Said R. Hoshaiah, "When the Holy One, blessed be he, came to create the first man, the ministering angels mistook him [for God, since man was in God's image,] and wanted to say before him, 'Holy, [holy, holy is the Lord of hosts].'

B. "To what may the matter be compared? To the case of a king and a governor who were set in a chariot, and the provincials wanted to greet the king, 'Sovereign!' But they did not know which one of them was which. What did the king do? He turned the governor out and put him away from the chariot, so that people would know who was king.

C. "So too when the Holy One, blessed be he, created the first man, the angels mistook him [for God]. What did the Holy One, blessed be he, do? He put him to sleep, so everyone knew that he was a mere man.

D. "That is in line with the following verse of Scripture: 'Cease you from man, in whose nostrils is a breath, for how little is he to be accounted' (Isa. 2:22)."

Genesis Rabbah VIII:X

In light of this reading of Genesis 1:9, we may hardly find surprising the power of diverse heirs of scripture, framers of various Judaic religious systems, to present portraits of the incarnation of God, corporeal, in affects and virtues consubstantial with humanity, doing things human beings do in the ways in which they do them.

Now it is clear, for most Christianities, Jesus Christ God Incarnate stands for a critical component of the faith; to undertake a dialogue with these Christianities, Judaic theologians will either speak to Christians as Christians or carry forward the Judaic part of the shared pretense, the hypocrisy of many centuries, that they mean to talk with someone whom, in fact, they do not wish even to acknowledge. When Judaic theologians bypass the conception of God Incarnate in Jesus Christ, they simply repeat the earlier insistence that Christianity never happened. To be sure, Christians mean various things by the notion of Incarnation. But a meaning probably acceptable to most Christianities is: "The union between divinity and humanity in the person of Jesus Christ."[1]

---

[1] Manabu Waida, "Incarnation," *Encyclopaedia of Religion* 7:156. Waida does not concur with Christian theology that the word "incarnation" can have only a capital I and refer only to Jesus Christ.

While in the contemporary Judeo-Christian dialogue, Christians pretend to find satisfying Judaic professions of admiration for the man ("but not what Christianity says about him"), matters in medieval times were more straightforward and blunt. Then, faced with the insistence that in Jesus Christ we know God Incarnate, Judaic partners to the dialogue conceded that they knew precisely what the Christians wished to say, and that it is nonsense.

Judaic respondents to Christian disputations in medieval times insisted the doctrine that any man, including Jesus, can be the incarnation of God defies all rationality. For the best instance, it is Maccoby who cites Nahmanides: "The doctrine in which you believe, the foundation of your faith, cannot be accepted by reason, nature affords no ground for it, nor have the prophets ever expressed it." No rational person can "believe such a doctrine: namely, that God Himself was born from a human womb, lived on earth and was executed, and then returned to His original place." Maccoby characterizes the Judaic objection as "clear infringement of the First Commandment."[2] The Messiah is not God incarnate, he is only a mortal man.

Nahmanides identifies, as the fundamental point of difference between Jews and Christians,

> what you say about the fundamental matter of the deity, a doctrine which is distasteful indeed . . . . : that the Creator of Heaven and earth resorted to the womb of a certain Jewish woman and grew there for nine months and was born as an infant and afterwards grew up and was betrayed into the hands of his enemies who sentenced him to death and persecuted him, and that afterwards . . . he came to life and returned to his original place. The mind of a Jew or any other person cannot tolerate this.[3]

---

[2]Hyam Maccoby, *Judaism on Trial: Jewish-Christian Disputations in the Middle Ages* (Rutherford, N.J.: Fairleigh Dickinson University Press, 1981), p. 54.

[3]Maccoby, pp. 119–120.

What is important to our problem is the insistence that such a
conception lies outside the bounds of human reason. It is simply inconceivable.

When we turn to the contemporary dialogue, we find
equally impressive candor (occasionally). For instance, our native speaker for contemporary Judaic discourse says, "Christianity is predicated on the doctrine of the incarnation: 'God
was in Christ, not in writing or doctrines or miracles or subjective experiences or sacramental forms, but in a historic person,
in Christ's spirit, his word, his life, his death.' And, she states
very simply, "Judaism . . . rejects Jesus as the son of God and
as an incarnation of the Divine Being[4] —elaborate demonstration that as soon as Judaic parties to a supposed Judeo-
Christian dialogue heard that the Christians believed Jesus
Christ was God Incarnate, they identified that as a critical component of Christianity and declared their judgment that that
belief is beyond comprehension.

At issue here, however, is not what Christianity says about
Jesus Christ or what Judaism responds. It is, Can we find in the
resources of Judaism a way of understanding what Christians
might mean when they speak of Jesus Christ God Incarnate?
If not, then, like Nahmanides for the medieval and Weiss-
Rosmarin for the modern Judaic parties to the dialogue, we
shall have to concur that honest dialogue with Christianity, on
matters important to Christianity, is simply not possible; we can
never find grounds for sympathetic hearing of what the Christians have to say. Therefore, whether or not we disagree with
them makes no difference at all; not understanding what they
wish to say in particular about Jesus—that is, Christ as God
Incarnate—whether we concur or do not concur has no bearing on dialogue; whatever we say, it will be in a language the
other party is not speaking. And whatever they say comes to us
in a language we cannot hear.

When, however, we ask whether in the resources of Judaism
we can understand what someone might mean in speaking of

[4]Trude Weiss-Rosmarin, *Judaism and Christianity: The Differences*
(New York: Jewish Book Club, 1943), p. 128.

God in human form and flesh—for that is what incarnation, the word, means—then matters change. For, among diverse candidates, two among many ways of seeing God in the authoritative canon of Judaism—that is, in the Torah—prepare us to say, Yes, that's what they're talking about, I can understand and sympathize with their feelings.

True, sympathy with feelings and attitudes does not lead to affirmation of doctrines and propositions; that God can be imagined, in line with the Torah, not only as a thin voice of silence, not only as a voice from beyond, but as a person with personality, says nothing about whether or not Jesus Christ—in particular, or alone and unique—was and is God in the flesh. That issue is not addressed, and outside of Christianity quite obviously it cannot be. But sympathy does bridge the gap between one side and the other, in that for Judaic believers what Christianity believes no longer has to be dismissed as beyond all rationality.

Do I then propose that, if Nahmanides read these lines and the evidence I shall presently set forth, and if he concurred (as I should fairly anticipate on solid grounds) that I have read the documents with care and accuracy and understand precisely what they mean, he would retract his judgment that the doctrine of Jesus Christ God Incarnate "cannot be accepted by reason, nature affords no ground for it, nor have the prophets ever expressed it"? Not at all (nor would I want him to). For he addressed not the human situation of Christianity, in quest of a sympathetic hearing of someone else's religion, but the aggressive insistence of Christianity that Judaism repudiate the Torah and accept Jesus as Christ God Incarnate or as Messiah or in any of the other legion of ways in which Jesus Christ formed the center of Christianity. His position took shape in a different intellectual (let alone political!) setting from that in which Judaism and Christianity today find themselves, along with Islam.

In his world Christianity maintained what it said was so, asking Judaism to grant not merely a sympathetic hearing, for the sake of mutual understanding and respect, but concession and submission to Christian truth. In that context, speaking out of the framework of Judaism, Nahmanides was entirely fair in saying about the point and the context in which the point was made: unreasonable, unfounded in nature, unsustained by the prophets. In his place I would have said the same thing, and in the context of evidence drawn from reason, nature, and scripture, I do concur, and I should hope every Jew in the world concurs. That is to say, in looking for evidence in the objective facts of reason, nature, and scripture, Nahmanides rightly found no support for the Christian view. What we want to find is not objective facts of reason or nature, but feelings and attitudes in scripture, the written Torah, and the oral Torah that will permit us to make sense of someone else's nonsense. That is a different vocation entirely.

What if the Christians had spoken not of Jesus Christ God Incarnate but only of the incarnation of God, meaning that God is like a human being? Then, I think, under benign circumstances, Nahmanides would have read the prophets with a different eye altogether. In his reading of the prophets, in particular, Abraham J. Heschel finds that the prophets disclosed attitudes of God: divine pathos.[5] What the prophets reveal about God tells us how God feels; he notes that

> they had an intuitive grasp of hidden meanings, of an unspoken message . . . the pensive-intuitive attitude of the prophet to God, in which God is apprehended through His sensible manifestations, is to be characterized as understanding . . . through the moment of revelation or through intuitive contemplation of the surrounding world; in the first case, they received an inspiration as an expression of the divine Person; in the second, they sensed the signs of God's presence in history."[6]

What the prophet knows, in particular, is how God is moved and affected by what happens in the world:

---

[5]Abraham J. Heschel, *The Prophets* (New York: Harper & Row, 1962), p. 221.

[6]Heschel, p. 222.

joy or sorrow, pleasure or wrath . . . he reacts in an intimate
and subjective manner . . . man's deeds may move Him, af-
fect Him, grieve Him, or gladden and please Him. This notion that God can be intimately affected, that He possesses
not merely intelligence and will, but also pathos, basically
defines the prophetic consciousness of God.[7]

God is not like humanity; human pathos yields passion; God's
pathos is "an act formed with intention . . . the result of deci-
sion and determination." Pathos is "not an attribute but a situation." Heschel carries this further:

The predicament of man is a predicament of God Who
has a stake in the human situation. Sin, guilt, suffering, cannot be separated from the divine situation. The life of sin is
more than a failure of man; it is a frustration to God. Thus
man's alienation from God is not the ultimate fact by which
to measure man's situation. The divine pathos, the fact of
God's participation in the predicament of man, is the ele-
mental fact.[8]

Heschel is explicit in that he speaks of not psychological pathos
but a theological connotation: God's involvement.

Humanity in God's image, in this context, is recast: "Man is
not only an image of God, he is a perpetual concern of God.
. . . Whatever man does affects not only his own life but also
the life of God insofar as it is directed to man. The import of
man raises him beyond the level of mere creature. He is con-
sort, a partner, a factor in the life of God."[9] True, God's pathos is not essence, "but a form of relation."[10] Were God
represented as wholly sharing the emotional responses of humanity, that is, as like humanity, then the conception of God
Incarnate in Jesus Christ would be irrelevant; God would be
incarnate in everyone equally, but no one especially.

Were God represented as wholly other, then neither Judaic

---

[7]Heschel, p. 224.
[8]Heschel, p. 226.
[9]Ibid.
[10]Heschel, p. 231.

nor Christian theology could entertain the notion of incarnation. It is this middle ground—pathos as relationship—that
permits Christians to speak of God Incarnate (in Jesus Christ)
to a sympathetic Judaic hearing. That is, very simply, while, as
Nahmanides said for all time, neither the facts of nature nor
reason sustain the conception of a God incarnate, prophecy
does set forth for Judaism the conception of a God consubstantial with humanity in the life of emotion and attitude, such
that God feels with us and for us. Now that prophetic view,
while in no way speaking of Jesus Christ God Incarnate, does
allow me to understand, in my framework, in my terms, in
accord with what the Torah says, what Christians might mean
when they speak, in their framework and in their terms, not of
God like us and us like God but, in very concrete terms, of this
man, God.

What appeal to the prophetic conception of divine pathos
yields, therefore, is what we seek: grounds in Judaism for understanding that to which Christians refer or may refer, a basis
for understanding what is otherwise (from our faith) outlandish
and absurd. I repeat, to say I can understand out of my experience what they might mean in their language is not to say I can
understand why Jesus Christ in particular is uniquely God Incarnate; the language of "uniqueness" leads us into the inner
heart of a religion, the point at which that religious system no
longer speaks to, or about, the other, but only in its intimacy
and privacy to God. There is no space there for the outsider.
My task is one of dialogue, not persuasion of the other to become like me, nor my conversion to the condition, the faith, of
the other.

When dialogue is at issue, we seek to understand, not to
persuade the other to concur with what I say, not to be persuaded of the truth the other says. Dialogue yields understanding; the condition of dialogue is autonomy, mutual and
reciprocal respect. On that basis, I repeat: divine pathos in the
prophets prepares me to see the conception of incarnation in a
Judaic light: we are like God in that God's feelings correspond
to ours, God's feelings respond to ours, and our feelings prepare us in some ways to understand God. That is not the doc-

trine of incarnation of any Christianity; it is only a view of incarnation that renders the conception of God in human form entirely congruent to the prophetic encounter that forms Judaic understanding of God.

Now, to pursue this same inquiry into the Judaic resources for the understanding of one of Christianity's critical beliefs, to us its most ridiculous, we move onward from the written Torah's prophetic record to the oral Torah's rabbinic one. As a matter of fact, in the final stage in the formation of the canon of the Judaism of the dual Torah, the incarnation of God forms a principal aspect of the character of divinity. Prior to that time, the character of divinity extended to portraits of God as (1) premise, the one who created the world and gave the Torah; (2) presence, supernatural being resident in the Temple and present where two or more persons engaged in discourse concerning the Torah; and (3) person, the one to whom prayer is addressed. But at the end we find important allusions to the incarnation of God as well as narratives that realize in concrete terms the incarnation of God. What is important to us is that when God is incarnate for Judaism, it is through stories about what God is and does that the knowledge of God reaches us. When I pointed to sharing our stories with each other as a means of gaining sympathy for what is alien about the other, I had in mind Talmudic stories about the incarnate God. These we tell ourselves. When we hear Christians' stories, we hear different stories, but we can respond to our stories in ways that accord with their response to their stories: a different kind of dialogue, but one I think is plausible.

In the present context, what exactly do I mean by a story that presents the incarnation of God? I mean the description of God, whether in allusion or narrative, as (1) corporeal; (2) exhibiting traits of emotions like those of human beings; (3) doing deeds women and men do, in the way in which they do them. When Christianity wants to tell what God is when incarnate, it points to Jesus Christ: corporeal, sharing the feelings of human beings, doing things women and men do, in the way in which they do them—yet God. The Talmud of Babylonia, the Bavli, the final statement of the formative period of the Juda-

ism of the dual Torah, represented God in the flesh in the
analogy of the human person. Prior to the Bavli, the faithful
encountered God as abstract premise, as unseen presence, as a
"you" without richly defined traits of soul, body, spirit, mind,
or feeling. The Bavli's authorship for the first time in the formation of Judaism presented God as a fully formed personality,
like a human being in corporeal traits, attitudes, emotions, and
other virtues, in actions and the means of carrying out actions.
God then looked the way human beings look, felt and responded the way they do, and did the actions they do in the
ways in which they do them. And yet in that portrayal of the
character of divinity, God always remained God.

The insistent comparison of God with humanity "in our image and likeness" comes to its conclusion in one sentence that
draws humanity upward and does not bring God downward.
For, despite its treatment of the sage as a holy man, the Bavli's
characterization of God never confused God with a sage or a
sage with God. Quite to the contrary, the point and purpose of
that characterization reaches its climax in a story that in powerful language demands that in the encounter with the sage of all
sages God be left to be God: *Silence, for that is how I have decided
matters.* When we reach that point, we shall have come to the
end of my account of the incarnation of God. Beyond that
point, for the formation of Judaism in its classic, normative,
and authoritative statement, is only silence.

The claim that the character of God is shaped in the model
of a human being requires substantiation: first of all, in quite
physical traits, such as are taken for granted in the passage just
now cited. Incarnation means precisely that: representation of
God in the flesh, as a human being, in the present context as a
man. We begin with a clear statement that has God represented
as a man,[11] seen in the interpretation of the vision of the
prophet Zechariah:

---

[11] I cannot point to a single representation of God in the feminine
in the literature under survey, but, of course, the potentiality was
present from scriptural writings onward, and a feminine dimension of

A. And said R. Yohanan, "What is the meaning of the verse of Scripture, 'I saw by night, and behold, a man riding upon a red horse, and he stood among the myrtle trees that were in the bottom' (Zech. 1:8)?

B. "What is the meaning of, 'I saw by night'?

C. "The Holy One, blessed be he, sought to turn the entire world into night.

D. " 'And behold, a man riding'—'man' refers only to the Holy One, blessed be he, as it is said, 'The Lord is a man of war; the Lord is his name' (Ex. 15:3).

E. " 'On a red horse'—the Holy One, blessed be he, sought to turn the entire world to blood.

F. "When, however, he saw Hananiah, Mishael, and Azariah, he cooled off, as it is said, 'And he stood among the myrtle trees that were in the deep.' "

Babylonian Talmud Sanhedrin 1:1.XLII [93A]

Scripture of course knows that God has a face, upon which human beings are not permitted to gaze. But was that face understood in a physical way, and did God enjoy other physical characteristics? An affirmative answer emerges entirely clearly in the following:

A. "And he said, 'You cannot see my face' (Ex. 33:20)."

B. It was taught on Tannaite authority in the name of R. Joshua b. Qorha, "This is what the Holy One, blessed be he, said to Moses:

C. " 'When I wanted [you to see my face], you did not want to, now that you want to see my face, I do not want you to.' "

D. This differs from what R. Samuel bar Nahmani said R. Jonathan said.

E. For R. Samuel bar Nahmani said R. Jonathan said, "As a reward for three things he received the merit of three things.

God is revealed in later writings.

F.   "As a reward for: 'And Moses hid his face' (Ex. 3:6), he had the merit of having a glistening face.

G.   "As a reward for: 'Because he was afraid' (Ex. 3:6), he had the merit that 'They were afraid to come near him' (Ex. 34:30).

H.   "As a reward for: 'To look upon God' (Ex. 3:6), he had the merit: 'The similitude of the Lord does he behold' (Num. 12:8)."

A.   "And I shall remove my hand and you shall see my back" (Ex. 33:23).

B.   Said R. Hana bar Bizna said R. Simeon the Pious, "This teaches that the Holy One, blessed be he, showed Moses [how to tie] the knot of the phylacteries."

Babylonian Talmud Berakot 7A, LVI

The incarnation of God encompassed not only physical but also emotional or attitudinal traits. In the final stage of the Judaism of the dual Torah, God emerged as a fully exposed personality. The character of divinity, therefore, encompassed God's virtue, the specific traits of character and personality that God exhibited above and here below. Above all, humility, the virtue sages most often asked of themselves, characterized the divinity. God wanted people to be humble, and God therefore showed humility.

A.   Said R. Joshua b. Levi, "When Moses came down from before the Holy One, blessed be he, Satan came and asked [God], 'Lord of the world, Where is the Torah?' "

B.   "He said to him, 'I have given it to the earth . . . ' [Satan ultimately was told by God to look for the Torah by finding the son of Amram].

C.   "He went to Moses and asked him, 'Where is the Torah which the Holy One, blessed be he, gave you?'

D.   "He said to him, 'Who am I that the Holy One, blessed be he, should give me the Torah?'

E.   "Said the Holy One, blessed be he, to Moses, 'Moses, you are a liar!'

F.   "He said to him, 'Lord of the world, you have a treasure in store which you have enjoyed every day. Shall I keep
it to myself?'

G.   "He said to him, 'Moses, since you have acted with
humility, it will bear your name: "Remember the Torah of
Moses, my servant" (Mal. 3:22).' "

Babylonian Talmud Shabbat 89a

God here is represented as favoring humility and rewarding the
humble with honor. What is important is that God does not
here cite scripture or merely paraphrase it; the conversation is
an exchange between two vivid personalities. True enough, Moses, not God, is the hero. But the personality of God emerges
in a vivid way. The following passage shows how traits imputed
to God also define proper conduct for sages, not to mention
other human beings.

The paramount trait of the sage in the Bavli is his profound
engagement with the life of Israel, God's people. The sage conducts an ongoing love affair with Israel, just as does God, caring for everything that Jews say and do, the sanctity of their
community, the holiness of their homes. Israel, unique among
nations and holy to God, forms on earth a society that corres-
ponds to the retinue and court of God in heaven. No surprise,
then, that just as Israel glorifies God, so God responds and
celebrates Israel. In the passages at hand the complete incarnation of God, in physical, emotional, and social traits, comes to
expression. God wears phylacteries, an indication of a corporeal sort. God further forms the correct attitude toward Israel,
which is one of love, an indication of an attitude on the part of
divinity corresponding to right attitudes on the part of human
beings. Finally, to close the circle, just as there is a "you" to
whom humanity prays, so God too says prayers—to God—and
the point of these prayers is that God should elicit from himself
forgiveness for Israel:

A.   Said R. Nahman bar Isaac to R. Hiyya bar Abin, "As
to the phylacteries of the Lord of the world, what is written
in them?"

B.   He said to him, " 'And who is like your people Israel, a singular nation on earth?' (1 Chr. 17:21)."

C.   "And does the Holy One, blessed be he, sing praises for Israel?"

D.   "Yes, for it is written, 'You have avouched the Lord this day . . . and the Lord has avouched you this day' (Deut. 26:17, 18).

E.   "Said the Holy One, blessed be he, to Israel, 'You have made me a singular entity in the world, and I shall make you a singular entity in the world.

F.   " 'You have made me a singular entity in the world,' as it is said, 'Hear, O Israel, the Lord, our God, the Lord is one' (Deut. 6:4).

G.   " 'And I shall make you a singular entity in the world,' as it is said, 'And who is like your people, Israel, a singular nation in the earth?' (1 Chr. 17:21)."

H.   Said R. Aha, son of Raba, to R. Ashi, "That takes care of one of the four subdivisions of the phylactery. What is written in the others?"

I.   He said to him, " 'For what great nation is there. . . . And what great nation is there . . . ' (Deut. 4:7, 8), 'Happy are you, O Israel . . . ' (Deut. 33:29), 'Or has God tried . . . ,' (Deut. 4:34). And 'To make you high above all nations' (Deut. 26:19)."

J.   "If so, there are too many boxes!"

K.   "But the verses, 'For what great nation is there' and 'And what great nation is there,' which are equivalent, are in one box, and 'Happy are you, O Israel' and 'Who is like your people Israel' are in one box, and 'Or has God tried . . . ,' in one box, and 'To make you high' in one box.

L.   "And all of them are written in the phylactery that is on the arm."

Babylonian Talmud Berakot 6A–B, XXXIX

A.   Said R. Yohanan in the name of R. Yosé, "How do we know that the Holy One, blessed be he, says prayers?

B. "Since it is said, 'Even them will I bring to my holy mountain and make them joyful in my house of prayer' (Isa. 56:7).

C. " 'Their house of prayer' is not stated, but rather, 'my house of prayer.'

D. "On the basis of that usage we see that the Holy One, blessed be he, says prayers."

E. "What prayers does he say?"

F. Said R. Zutra bar Tobiah said Rab, " 'May it be my will that my mercy overcome my anger, and that my mercy prevail over my attributes, so that I may treat my children in accord with the trait of mercy and in their regard go beyond the strict measure of the law.' "

Babylonian Talmud Berakot 7A, XLIX

A. It has been taught on Tannaite authority:

B. Said R. Ishmael b. Elisha, "One time I went in to offer up incense on the innermost altar, and I saw the crown of the Lord, enthroned on the highest throne, and he said to me, 'Ishmael, my son, bless me.'

C. "I said to him, 'May it be your will that your mercy overcome your anger, and that your mercy prevail over your attributes, so that you treat your children in accord with the trait of mercy and in their regard go beyond the strict measure of the law.'

D. "And he nodded his head to me."

E. And from that story we learn that the blessing of a common person should not be negligible in your view.

Babylonian Talmud Berakot 7A, L

The process of the incarnation of God culminates in the portrait of God as Israel's counterpart, trait by trait, and in all relationships: God unique in heaven, Israel unique on earth, the one like the other and matched only by the other.

How then is the Incarnate God represented by the oral Torah? This story treats the incarnation of God:

A.   Said R. Judah said Rab, "When Moses went up to the height, he found the Holy One, blessed be he, sitting and tying crowns to the letters [of the Torah]."

B.   "He said to him, 'Lord of the universe, why is this necessary?'

C.   "He said to him, 'There is a certain man who is going to come into being at the end of some generations, by the name of Aqiba b. Joseph. He is going to find expositions to attach mounds and mounds of laws to each point [of a crown].'

D.   "He said to him, 'Lord of the universe, show him to me.'

E.   "He said to him, 'Turn around.'

F.   "[Moses] went and took his seat at the end of eight rows, but he could not understand what the people were saying. He felt weak. When discourse came to a certain matter, one of [Aqiba's] disciples said to him, 'My lord, how do you know this?'

G.   "He said to him, 'It is a law revealed by God to Moses at Mount Sinai.'

H.   "Moses' spirits were restored.

I.   "He turned back and returned to the Holy One, blessed be he. He said to him, 'Lord of the universe, now if you have such a man available, how can you give the Torah through me?'

J.   "He said to him, 'Be silent. That is how I have decided matters.'

K.   "He said to him, 'Lord of the universe, you have now shown me his mastery of the Torah. Now show me his reward.'

L.   "He said to him, 'Turn around.'

M.   "He turned around and saw people weighing out his flesh in the butcher-shop.

N.   "He said to him, 'Lord of the universe, such is his mastery of Torah, and such is his reward?'

O.   "He said to him, 'Be silent. That is how I have decided matters.' "

Babylonian Talmud Menahot 29B

The story is open-ended: "Be silent. That is how I have decided matters." That statement hardly marks a happy ending, and it assuredly does not answer the question with which the passage commences. The story merely restates the question in a more profound way. So the one truly striking story about God in the form of not a human being in general but a sage in particular, a sage engaged in debate and argument, turns out to make precisely the opposite of the point of every other sage story. All other such stories tell us how sages resolve points of tension and sort out conflict, bringing to a happy resolution whatever problem has generated the action of the story. But this story tells us the precise opposite, which is that God decrees and even the sage—even our rabbi, Moses, the sage of all sages— must maintain humble silence and accept the divine decree. Turning matters around in a secular direction, we may state the proposition in this way: The sage is like God but, like all other human beings, subject to God's ultimately autocephalic decree.

A story built on the premise of the incarnation of God, fully exposing God's traits of personality and portraying God like a sage, engaged in argument with a man as the master engages in argument with a disciple, serves a stunning purpose, which contradicts its academic form. It is to show that God, while like a sage, is more than a sage—much more. And even in this deeply human context, that "more" is to be stated only in the submission expressed through silence. This I take to be the final statement of the incarnation of God of the Judaism of the dual Torah. God incarnate remains God ineffable. When the Judaism of the dual Torah wishes to portray the character of divinity, it invokes in the end the matter of relationship and not tactile quality and character. If we wish to know God, it is through our relationship to God, not through our (entirely legitimate and welcome) act of the incarnation of God in heart and mind and soul, deliberation and deed. And the way to engage with, relate to, God, in the face of (in the suggestive instance at hand) the Torah and the torture of Aqiba, is silence.

So, for the faithful Jew, is the conception of God incarnate beyond all reason, ridiculous, absurd? Not at all. When I tell my stories, in which I learn how the Torah reveals God, both the stories of the prophets and what God said to them, and the stories of our sages of blessed memory and how they knew God in incarnate form, I can understand how someone else may tell stories about God in us, and about how we can become like God. Can I then listen with sympathy to the Christian story of Jesus Christ God Incarnate? Without doubt: I can listen with sympathy, because the Torah teaches me how. Do I have to listen to such stories? If I want to know how to understand my stories better, that is to say, to think deeply about what it means for us to be like God, about what it means for humanity to incarnate God—for "incarnate" is a transitive verb—then to open my heart and soul to all the ways people can imagine God incarnate, I do. That is, to know what it means to be human "like God," I do well to listen to the stories other people tell too, about what it means to be "in our image, after our like-ness," as their hearts and minds have told the story to them.

8

A Christian Telling of the Judaic Tale— Israel Instead of Adam: Christian Resources for Imagining Israel

When Christians hear the word "Israel," they think first of the state of Israel, then of the people of Israel in biblical times. Identifying with ancient Israel through the Old Testament, Christians inherit another conception of Israel as well, one that makes a sympathetic response to the state of Israel parlous. It is, as we have already noticed, the notion that the destruction of the Temple and the end of the Jewish state in 70 punished Israel "after the flesh," and until the Jews today repent and accept Christ, they should have no state. The creation of the state of Israel in 1948, in the aftermath of the murder of most of the Jews in Christian Europe, called into question a long-held conviction; the state further formed an embarrassment to Christian Arabs, on the one side, and to Christian missions and institutions in Muslim countries, on the other.

When, therefore, Judaic participants to the Judeo-Christian dialogue raise the question of Christian hostility to the state of Israel, the Christian partners find very difficult the intrusion of a political question into a religious dialogue; what, after all, can be "religious" about a secular state? And that objection under-lines yet another ongoing Christian difficulty in making sense of the Jews, which is the Jews' intense sense of "being Jewish," whether or not a professed religious conviction about "being holy Israel" infuses that "being Jewish" with religious content. The fusion of the ethnic, the religious, the cultural, and the political presents woeful confusion to Christians. But there is no dialogue with Israel, the Jewish people, without a clear Christian understanding of what, in Judaism, "Israel" stands for, and why, for nearly all Jews, there is no sorting out the religious, ethnic, and cultural categories—not to mention, after all, the genealogical as well. For Jews the given of our existence, "Israel" in all its dimensions, involving the state, the land, the people there and everywhere, stands as an obstacle to dialogue for Christians.

"Israel" forms a considerable obstacle to Judeo-Christian dialogue, for Christian theological reasons. And these form as central a component of Christian theology as do those beliefs that render the conception of an Incarnate God exceedingly difficult for Judaism. To provide a single example of how a Christian thinker dealt with Israel, let me refer to Aphrahat's *Demonstration Sixteen, "On the Peoples which are in the Place of the People."* Aphrahat's message is this:

> The people Israel was rejected, and the peoples took their place. Israel repeatedly was warned by the prophets, but to no avail, so God abandoned them and replaced them with the gentiles. Scripture frequently referred to the gentiles as "Israel." The vocation of the peoples was prior to that of the people of Israel, and from of old, whoever from among the people was pleasing to God was more justified than Israel: Jethro, the Gibeonites, Rahab, Ebedmelech the Ethiopian, Uriah the Hittite. By means of the gentiles God provoked Israel.

It suffices to point to a few important components of the argument. First, Aphrahat maintains, "The peoples which were of all languages were called first, before Israel, to the inheritance of the Most High, as God said to Abraham, 'I have made you the father of a multitude of peoples' (Gen. 17:5). Moses proclaimed, saying, 'The peoples will call to the mountain, and there will they offer sacrifices of righteousness' (Deut. 33:19)." Not only so, but God further rejected Israel:

To his people Jeremiah preached, saying to them, "Stand by the ways and ask the wayfarers, and see which is the good way. Walk in it." But they in their stubbornness answered, saying to him, "We shall not go." Again he said to them, "I established over you watchmen, that you might listen for the sound of the trumpet." But they said to him again, "We shall not hearken." And this openly, publicly did they do in the days of Jeremiah when he preached to them the word of the Lord, and they answered him, saying, "To the word which you have spoken to us in the name of the Lord we shall not hearken. But we shall do our own will and every word which goes out of our mouths, to offer up incense-offerings to other gods" (Jer. 44:16–17).

That is why God turned to the peoples: "When he saw that they would not listen to him, he turned to the peoples, saying to them, 'Hear, O peoples, and know, O church which is among them, and hearken, O land, in its fullness' (Jer. 6:18–19)." So who is now Israel? It is the peoples, no longer the old Israel: "By the name of Jacob [now] are called the people which is of the peoples." That is the key to Aphrahat's case. The people that was no-people, that people that had assembled out of the people, has now replaced Israel.

Like Eusebius, Aphrahat maintained that the peoples had been called to God before the people of Israel:

See, my beloved, that the vocation of the peoples was recorded before the vocation of the people. But because the time of the peoples had not come, and another was [to be] their redeemer, Moses was not persuaded that a redeemer and a teacher would come for the people which was of the peoples, which was greater and more worthy than the people of Israel.

The people that was no-people should not regard itself as alien to God: "If they should say, 'Us has he called alien children,' they have not been called alien children, but sons and heirs. . . . But the peoples are those who hearken to God and were lamed and kept back from the ways of their sins." Indeed, the

peoples produced believers who were superior in every respect
to Israel: "Even from the old, whoever from among the peoples was pleasing to God was more greatly justified than Israel.
Jethro the priest who was of the peoples and his seed were
blessed: 'Enduring is his dwelling place, and his nest is set on a
rock' (Num. 24:21)." Aphrahat here refers to the Gibeonites,
Rahab, and various other gentiles mentioned in the scriptural
narrative.

Addressing his Christian hearers, Aphrahat then continues,

> By us they are provoked. On our account they do not wor-
> ship idols, so that they will not be shamed by us, for we have
> abandoned idols and call lies the thing which our fathers left
> us. They are angry, their hearts are broken, for we have
> entered and have become heirs in their place. For theirs was
> this covenant which they had, not to worship other gods, but
> they did not accept it. By means of us he provoked them,
> and ours was the light and the life, as he preached, saying
> when he taught, "I am the light of the world" (John 8:12).

So he concludes,

> This brief memorial I have written to you concerning the
> peoples, because the Jews take pride and say, "We are the
> people of God and the children of Abraham." But we shall
> listen to John [the Baptist] who, when they took pride [say-
> ing], "We are the children of Abraham," then said to them,
> "You should not boast and say, Abraham is father unto us,
> for from these very rocks can God raise up children for
> Abraham" (Matt. 3:9).

In *Demonstration Nineteen, "Against the Jews, on account of their
saying that they are destined to be gathered together,"* Aphrahat
proceeds to the corollary argument, that Israel after the flesh
has lost its reason to endure as a nation. Why? Because no
salvation awaits in the future. The prophetic promises of salvation have all come to fulfillment in the past, and the climactic
salvation for Israel, through the act of Jesus Christ, brought
the salvific drama to its conclusion. Hence the Jews' not having
a hope of "joining together" at the end of their exile forms a

critical part of the entire picture. Here is a summary of the argument:

> The Jews expect to be gathered together by the Messiah, but this expectation is in vain. God was never reconciled to them but has rejected them. The prophetic promises of restoration were all fulfilled in the return from Babylonia. Daniel's prayer was answered, and his vision was realized in the time of Jesus and in the destruction of Jerusalem. It will never be rebuilt.

Aphrahat thus stresses that the Jews' sins caused their own condition, a position which sages accepted: "On account of their sins, which were many, he uprooted and scattered them among every nation, for they did not listen to his prophets, whom he had sent to them." The Jews now maintain that they will see salvation in the future, but they are wrong. "I have written this to you because even today they hope an empty hope, saying, 'It is still certain for Israel to be gathered together,' for the prophet thus spoke, 'I shall leave none of them among the nations' (Ex. 39:28). But if all of our people is to be gathered together, why are we today scattered among every people?" But, Aphrahat states, "Israel never is going to be gathered together." The reason is that God was never reconciled to Israel: "I shall write and show you that never did God accept their repentance [through] either Moses or all of the prophets. . . . Further, Jeremiah said, 'They are called rejected silver, for the Lord has rejected them' (Jer. 6:30). . . . See, then, they have never accepted correction in their lives."

Aphrahat presents an array of prophetic proof texts for the same proposition. Then he turns to the peoples and declares that they have taken the place of the people:

> Concerning the vocation of the peoples Isaiah said, "It shall come to be in the last days that the mountain of the House of the Lord will be established at the head of the mountains and high above the heights. Peoples will come together to it, and many peoples will go and say, Come, let us go up to the mountain of the Lord, to the House of the God of Jacob.

> He will teach us his ways, and we shall walk in his paths. For from Zion the law will go forth, and the word of the Lord from Jerusalem" (Isa. 2:2–3).

Does Israel not hope for redemption in the future? Indeed so, but they are wrong:

> Two times only did God save Israel: Once from Egypt, the second time from Babylonia; from Egypt by Moses, and from Babylonia by Ezra and by the prophecy of Haggai and Zechariah. Haggai said, "Build this house, and I shall have pleasure in it, and in it I shall be glorified, says the Lord" (Hag. 1:8). . . . All of these things were said in the days of Zerubbabel, Haggai, and Zechariah. They were exhorting concerning the building of the house.

The house was built—and then destroyed, and it will not be rebuilt. (Aphrahat wrote before Julian's proposed rebuilding of the temple, so he could not have derived further proof from that disaster).

I have dwelt on Aphrahat's doctrine of Israel not because he is influential but because, in a corner of the Christian world, he formulated views that typify broadly held Christian doctrine. And, from the beginnings to the present, that doctrine has put down such deep roots that nearly everywhere, if Jews were present, it was as alien intruders, tolerated, accorded sufferance at best.

So much for the challenge of those who held such views as Aphrahat expresses. The case is complete: the people which is no-people, the people which is of the peoples, have taken the place of the people that claims to carry forward the salvific history of ancient Israel. The reason is in two complementary parts. First, Israel has rejected salvation and so lost its reason to exist, and, second, the no-people have accepted salvation and so gained its reason to exist. So the threads of the dispute link into a tight fabric: the shift in the character of politics, marked by the epochal triumph of Christianity in the state, bears profound meaning for the messianic mission of the church and, further, imparts a final judgment on the salvific claim of the competing nations of God: the church and Israel.

Not a Christian, I am hardly to be expected to explain for Christians, out of the resources of Christianity, the Judaic theory of Israel. Were I to attempt to do so, I should place myself above the dialogue, like God, the arbiter of conflicting claims, when, in simple fact, I ask only to take my stand on the Judaic side of a conversation I hope to make possible. What I can attempt is to explain to Christians in Judaic terms what "Israel" stands for, in the hope that Christians may find sympathy for our "Israel" by appeal to three profoundly Christian concepts. These, then, must be specified to begin with.

First comes the theory that, from the fall of Adam, humanity arose from the dregs of sin through Christ. In Romans 1–3, Paul explains how no human being escapes the domination of sin. The human condition is defined by the first sin, Adam and Eve's, so sin is natural to the human condition.

Then Paul contrasts the first Adam, source of death, to Christ, the second Adam, source of life:

> For as by a man came death, by a man has come also the resurrection of the dead. For as in Adam all die, so also in Christ shall all be made alive. But each in his own order: Christ the first fruits, then at his coming those who belong to Christ (1 Cor. 15:21–22).

> The first man Adam became a living being; the last Adam became a life-giving spirit (1 Cor. 15:45).

> The first man was from the earth, a man of dust, the second man is from heaven. As was the man of dust, so are those who are of the dust; and as is the man of heaven, so are those who are of heaven. Just as we have borne the image of the man of dust, we shall also bear the image of the man of heaven (1 Cor. 15:47–49).

In the Judaism of the dual Torah, "Israel" serves precisely in the same way—that is, marking the rise of humanity from the fall of Adam to the pinnacle: of Sinai.

The second and third points come together. On the one side, as Hebrews says in so many words, this atonement for sin was achieved through Christ's suffering. On the other side, Christ stands for the suffering servant of Isaiah:

> He was oppressed, and he was afflicted, yet he opened not his mouth; like a lamb that is led to the slaughter, and like a sheep that before its shearers is dumb, so he opened not his mouth.
>
> By oppression and judgment he was taken away; and as for his generation, who considered that he was cut off out of the land of the living, stricken for the transgression of my people? (Isa. 53:7–8)

Christians will not find Judaism's—and the Jews'—conception of "Israel" so absurd if, in sympathy, they can understand a simple fact. *There is scarcely a Jew in the world who reads these words without understanding, beyond all doubt, that when Isaiah spoke he told us about the Holocaust.*

Do I mean, then, to suggest that Christianity now contemplate substituting "Israel" for "Christ"? Of course not, any more than I should want Judaism to make sense of nonsense and therefore consider Jesus Christ God Incarnate to stand for what God meant when God spoke of us "in our image, after our likeness." Just as I seek in the resources of Judaism to find foundations for sympathy for a profoundly alien conception of the other, so I hope that out of the resources of Christianity— not merely out of sentimentality or a sense of shame or (misplaced) guilt for the Christian contribution to the murder of Jewry in Christendom—Christians may seek some sense of what they see as the Judaic nonsense about this "Israel."

To begin with, of course, within the framework of the Bible "Israel" stands for God's people, and when the church determined to define "the Bible" as both the Old and the New Testaments, as it did, then the church confirmed, for mainstream Christianity, all that the Torah had said about Israel. At issue was only whether or not the Jews after Calvary and Easter were that "Israel" of which the scriptures had spoken, or whether there now was a new "Israel," which excluded the old. The heart of the matter of "Israel," then, was—and, I insist, remains!—whether or not we Jews form the Israel of whom scripture speaks. We have never, ever, imagined otherwise. But important Christian theologians have denied it. And, in point of fact, that denial of what is for Jews a component of the faith as critical as the figure of Christ itself—our -ism, after all, is Judaism, that is, the -ism of Judah, or the Jews, while the Christians' -ity is the -ity of Christ, Christian-ity—cuts to the core. And to that point at issue—are we still "Israel," as we insist, or is there now a "new Israel" to the exclusion of the old?—the Jewishness of Jesus, the Christian reverence for the "Old Testament," the conception that "spiritually, we are all Semites," and other expressions meant as goodwill but in fact stating little more than condescension—all these platitudes of the dialogue to date are monumentally irrelevant. What we claim as "Israel" is so encompassing and fundamental to our being that, in all candor, Christians' cordial insistence that Jesus was ("after all") a Jew too (so therefore we don't really loathe you as much as we would otherwise) proves little less than presumptuous.

For, in the theory of "Israel" put forward by Judaism, we shall now see, our "Israel" serves like the Christian Christ: the antidote to Adam:

2. A. "And they heard the sound of the Lord God walking in the garden in the cool of the day" (Gen. 3:8): Said R. Abba bar Kahana, "The word is not written, 'move,' but rather, 'walk,' bearing the sense that [the Presence of God] leapt about and jumped upward.

B. "[The point is that God's presence leapt upward from the earth on account of the events in the garden, as will now be explained:] The principal location of the Presence of God was [meant to be] among the creatures down here. When the first man sinned, the Presence of God moved up to the first firmament. When Cain sinned, it went up to the second firmament. When the generation of Enosh sinned, it went up to the third firmament. When the generation of the Flood sinned, it went up to the fourth firmament. When the generation of the dispersion [at the tower of Babel] sinned, it went up to the fifth. On account of the Sodomites it went up to the sixth, and on account of the Egyptians in the time of Abraham it went up to the seventh.

C.   "But, as a counterpart, there were seven righteous men who rose up: Abraham, Isaac, Jacob, Levi, Kahath, Amram, and Moses. They brought the Presence of God [by stages] down to earth.

D.   "Abraham brought it from the seventh to the sixth, Isaac brought it from the sixth to the fifth, Jacob brought it from the fifth to the fourth, Levi brought it down from the fourth to the third, Kahath brought it down from the third to the second, Amram brought it down from the second to the first. Moses brought it down to earth."

Genesis Rabbah to Genesis 3:1–13, XIX:VII

God left the world with Adam's sin; Abraham, Isaac, Jacob, and onward to Moses at Sinai brought God back to the world. More to the point, as we shall now see, the life of Israel in the Land of Israel forms a counterpoint and opposite to the life of Adam in the Garden of Eden. Israel is the successor to Adam, what God brought about in opposition to Adam.

2.   A.   R. Abbahu in the name of R. Yose bar Haninah: "It is written, 'But they are like a man [Adam], they have transgressed the covenant' (Hos. 6:7).

B.   " 'They are like a man,' specifically, like the first man. [We shall now compare the story of the first man in Eden with the story of Israel in its land.]

C.   " 'In the case of the first man, I brought him into the garden of Eden, I commanded him, he violated my commandment, I judged him to be sent away and driven out, but I mourned for him, saying "How . . . " '[which begins the book of Lamentations, hence stands for a lament, but which, as we just saw, also is written with the consonants that yield, 'Where are you'].

D.   " 'I brought him into the garden of Eden,' as it is written, 'And the Lord God took the man and put him into the garden of Eden' (Gen. 2:15).

E.   " 'I commanded him,' as it is written, 'And the Lord God commanded . . . ' (Gen. 2:16).

F.   " 'And he violated my commandment,' as it is written, 'Did you eat from the tree concerning which I commanded you?' (Gen. 3:11).

G.   " 'I judged him to be sent away,' as it is written, 'And
the Lord God sent him from the garden of Eden' (Gen.
3:23).

H.   " 'And I judged him to be driven out.' 'And he drove
out the man' (Gen. 3:24).

I.   " 'But I mourned for him, saying, "How . . . ." ' ' 'And
he said to him, "Where are you?" ' (Gen. 3:9), and the word
for 'where are you' is written, 'How. . . . '

J.   " 'So too in the case of his descendants, [God continues to speak,] I brought them into the Land of Israel, I
commanded them, they violated my commandment, I
judged them to be sent out and driven away but I mourned
for them, saying, "How. . . . " '

K.   " 'I brought them into the Land of Israel.' 'And I
brought you into the land of Carmel' (Jer. 2:7).

L.   " 'I commanded them.' 'And you, command the children of Israel' (Ex. 27:20). 'Command the children of Israel'
(Lev. 24:2).

M.   " 'They violated my commandment.' 'And all Israel
have violated your Torah' (Dan. 9:11).

N.   " 'I judged them to be sent out.' 'Send them away,
out of my sight and let them go forth' (Jer 15:1).

O.   " ' . . . and driven away.' 'From my house I shall
drive them' (Hos. 9:15).

P.   " 'But I mourned for them, saying, "How. . . . " '
'How has the city sat solitary, that was full of people' (Lam.
1:1)."

Genesis Rabbah to Genesis 3:8, XIX:IX

I find deeply moving the comparison of the story of man in
the Garden of Eden with the tale of Israel in its Land. Every
detail is in place, the articulation is perfect, and the result com-
pletely convinces as an essay in interpretation. All of this rests
on the simple fact that the word for "where are you" may be
expressed as "How . . . ," which, as is clear, invokes the open-

ing words of the book of Lamentations. What is important to
us is the representation of Israel: Israel's history serves as a
paradigm for human history, and vice versa.

Then Israel stands at the center of humanity. And "Israel"
forms a theological category, like "Christ," in this context, for
Paul:

> For as by Adam came death, by Israel will come also the
> resurrection of the dead. For as in Adam all die, so also in
> Israel [at the end of days], shall all be made alive.
>
> The first man Adam became a living being; the last
> Adam—read: Israel—became a life-giving spirit.

I cannot expect a Christian to concur; the reason is not that
the grammar does not work, since, as we see, the grammar
works to produce intelligible statements. But, for the Christian,
the recasting of Paul's statement is profoundly jarring, as dis-
ruptive as the claim that "in our image, after our likeness,"
refers to Christ Jesus. I claim only intelligibility; a nonsense
statement by sympathy, formed out of the resources of Christianity, can become a statement of sense: jarring, offensive,
wrong (as Nahmanides rightly told the king)—but at least intelligible. Can a Christian find sympathy for this Judaic "absurd-
ity," finding nonsense intelligible by reflection on what it
means to aver that Christ forms the counterpoint to Adam?
That is not for me to say.

The reason that, for Christians, as great an effort at sympathy is required to grasp our "Israel" as for us to grasp "Jesus
Christ God Incarnate" is that for them, as for many Jews, the
Jews are seen to form, in the context of the life of the Western
democracies, an ethnic group, and in the context of the nations
the state of Israel quite reasonably is understood as another
nation-state. Since, after all, no one has ever conceived of a
Presbyterian state beyond Calvin's Geneva, which hardly finds
a valid analogy in the state of Israel, so, when Jews speak of a
Jewish state, they must mean merely another state. The wit, the
just sense, of Zionism's (and all Jews') calling the Jewish state
"the state of Israel," meaning, first, what it means to be "Israel"; second, the nation-state that constitutes "Israel"; so,

therefore, the definition, for the here and now, of "Israel-ness," like all truly profound statements, lies right on the surface. But then, what are Christians to make of the religious meaning imputed in Judaism to this political (in one context) and ethnic (in the other context) entity?

Being "Israel" is physical, material, concrete. One becomes Israel after the flesh. It is the simple fact that the status of "Israel" passes through the physical body. Orthodox and Conservative Judaism define the Jew as a person born of a Jewish mother, and Reform Judaism as a person born of a Jewish mother or father. Here we confront what some call "the scandal of particularity." For Judaism speaks of "Israel," meaning the Jewish people—us in particular—as Christianity speaks of Christ, the mystical body of Christ, and "the church." That is, religious criteria operate too. And, as a matter of simple fact, a gentile who accepts the Torah enters that physical, material, fleshly Israel as well, so that the children of converts to Judaism are fully "Israel." The line between the supernatural social entity, called into being by God in God's service, and the this-worldly social group, formed by people of common background and culture, is a very fine one. In Judaism it is difficult to make out: not only after the flesh but also through what Christians would call "the spirit": that is, through "coming under the wings of the Presence of God," acceptance of the Torah and the religious duties, a gentile is transformed physically (circumcision and baptism for males, baptism for females). That ambiguity is not resolved; for Judaism, it cannot be, not being perceived as an ambiguity at all.

So, if you convert to the Roman Catholic religion, you do not automatically become Spanish, Italian, or Brazilian (to name three Roman Catholic nations), and if you become Episcopalian, you do not automatically get a British passport (or an English accent). But if you convert to Judaism, you automatically become a Jew, a member of the ethnic group. And, to flip the coin, no one ever called the Methodists a people, and there is no Presbyterian state, yet the Jews are called a people, there is a Jewish state, and the people and state identify the religion as their own.

The reason that Judaism and Christianity may find it possible to conduct an honest dialogue, in the form of a debate, is that we deal with a debate on a single issue. It finds its cogency in the common premise of the debate on who is Israel. The shared supposition has concerned God's favor and choice of a given entity, one that was *sui generis*, among the social groups of humanity. Specifically, both parties have concurred that God did favor and therefore make use of one group and not another, so they could undertake a meaningful debate on the identity of that group. The debate gains intensity because of a further peculiarity of the discourse between these two groups but no others, past or present (and one that, for contemporary reasons, really does exclude Islam). Both have concurred that the group chosen by God will bear the name Israel.

God's choice among human societies would settle the question, Which nation does God love and favor? Jews have seen, and now see themselves, as the Israel today joined in the flesh to the Israel of the scriptural record. Christians explained themselves as the Israel formed just now, in recent memory, even in the personal experience of the living, among those saved by faith in God's salvation afforded by the resurrection of Jesus Christ. We therefore must not miss the powerful social and political message conveyed by what appear to be statements of a narrowly theological character about salvation and society. In these statements on who is Israel, the parties to the debate chose to affirm each its own unique legitimacy and to deny the other's right to endure at all as a social and national entity.

Both parties share common premises as to definitions of issues and facts to settle the question. They can mount a sustained argument between themselves because they talked about the same thing, invoked principles of logic in common, shared the definition of the pertinent facts. They differ only as to the outcome. But the differences are very real, and much is at stake. That makes the problem, for Christianity, no less painful than the problem of Christ as God Incarnate for Judaism. For the issue of who is (the true) Israel articulated in theological, not political, terms covers several topics: Are the Jews today

"Israel" of ancient times? If so, who are the Christians, both on their own and also in relationship to ancient Israel? These questions scarcely can be kept distinct from one another. And all of them cover the ground we have already traversed concerning Christology (covered here, to be sure, in only one small aspect).

First was, and is, Jesus the Christ? If so, then the Jews who rejected him enjoyed no share in the salvation at hand. If not, then they do. The Christian challenge comes first. If Jesus was and is Christ, then Israel "after the flesh" no longer enjoys the status of the people who bear salvation. Salvation has come, and Israel "after the flesh" has denied it. If he is Christ, then what is the status of those—whether Jews or gentiles—who did accept him? They have received the promises of salvation and their fulfillment. The promises to Israel have been kept for them.

Then there is a new Israel, one that is formed of the saved, as the prophets had said in ancient times that Israel would be saved. A further issue that flows from the first—the rejection of Jesus as Christ—concerns the status of Israel, the Jewish people, now and in time to come. Israel after the flesh, represented from the Gospels forward as the people that rejected Jesus as Christ and participated in his crucifixion, claims to be the family of Abraham, Isaac, Jacob. Then further questions arise. First, does Israel today continue the Israel of ancient times? Israel maintains that Israel now continues in a physical and spiritual way the life of Israel then. Second, will the promises of the prophets to Israel afford salvation for Israel in time to come? Israel "after the flesh" awaits the fulfillment of the prophetic promise of salvation.

Clearly, this was a broad range of questions to sort out. But the questions flow together into a single issue, faced in common. The Christian position on all these questions came to expression in a single negative: no, Israel today does not continue the Israel of old; no, the ancient promises will not again bear salvation, because they have already been kept; so, the Israel that declines to accept Jesus' claim to be the Christ is no-people.

The scandal to the Jews—God incarnate indeed!—is now joined by the stumbling block to the other side—Israel indeed! What is critical to the one side finds its counterpart in what is critical to the other, and, we now realize, we have found our way to the heart of the matter of whether or not dialogue is at all possible (I mean a dialogue formed by an exchange of stories). In telling myself the story of Rachel, I find in the Torah resources of sympathy for what Roman Catholic Christianity believes about Mary; and in telling myself the story of God's pathos, of God adumbrated in the sage, I find less alien the Christian story of how God walked among us and showed us what it means to be (like) God.

I do not know the story that, within Christianity, will elicit sympathy for what "Israel" means to me. Christians may find useful a representation of "Israel" that is religious in the sense in which Christianity defines religion. First, "Israel" finds definition in relationship to its opposite. In so stating, sages (for example, in the Mishnah) did not merely describe a group; they portrayed it as they wished to. They did not assemble facts and define the social entity, the social group, as a matter of mere description of the given, on the basis of the pertinent ones. They imputed to the social group, Jews, the standing of the systemic entity, "Israel," and they assigned to that entity traits that, to begin with, form in the distant reaches of mind, such as belief in the resurrection of the dead as a scriptural doctrine. For to call a people a holy people, persons who did not, after all, see and know one another, to identify those persons in the here and now with that "Israel" of which scripture speaks—these seem to me daring acts of metaphorization, the most remarkable ones that we shall witness in the formative processes of the Judaism of the dual Torah. And the powerful argumentation assigned to the metaphorization of the social group consisted of treating as fact what was a statement of imagination, of poetry: always calling "Israel" the group, the individual, in the everyday world of mundane discourse of which the Mishnah is composed. The identification of Jewry in the here and now with the "Israel" of scripture constituted an act of metaphor, comparison, contrast, identification, and analogy, and I therefore point to "Israel" as that Judaism's most daring social metaphor.

The fact that through the ages it has seemed self-evident, a given of the Jews' everyday circumstance, shows us the success of the Judaism of the dual Torah, as much as seeing that metaphor as a choice among alternatives shows us the reason for that success. Seeing Jews and calling them "Israel"—an act of imaginative daring indeed—forms the metaphor that gives the system its energy, and from that metaphor all else derived its momentum. But the metaphor expanded, over time, with the view of "Israel" as a family, the children and heirs of the man, Israel; second, the conception of Israel as *sui generis*. "Israel" as a mere metaphor finds definition in relationship to its opposite, everybody else (as to "Christian" a natural antonym is "non-Christian"). But "Israel" as family, heirs of Abraham and Sarah and the rest of the patriarchs and matriarchs, transforms genealogy into theology, as Paul tried to do in Romans 9, invoking the metaphor of a branch grafted onto an olive tree. For in Judaism "Israel" stands for a real social group, not merely an entity in theory. And so too do churches, in comparison to the abstraction "the church." "Israel" forms a family, people who bear responsibility for one another, and this sense of family, spilling over from the theological and religious to the ethnic, assuredly will be sensible to Christians, who quite reasonably expect Christianity to instruct them on the requirements of the social order, beginning with home and family.

The correspondence of Christianity's Christ, or mystical body of Christ, or church, to Judaism's Israel explains why, for so long, Christianity has found incomprehensible Judaism's understanding of Israel. By claiming that "Israel" constituted "Israel after the flesh," the actual, living, present family of Abraham and Sarah, Isaac and Rebecca, Jacob and Leah and Rachel, sages met head-on the Christian claim that there was—or could ever be—some other "Israel," of a lineage not defined by the family connection at all, and that the existing Jews no longer constituted "Israel." By representing "Israel" as *sui generis,* sages moreover focused upon the systemic teleology, with its definition of salvation, in response to the Christian claim that salvation is not of Israel but of the church, now enthroned in this world as in heaven. The sage, model for Israel, in the model of Moses, our rabbi, on earth represented the Torah that had come from heaven. Like Christ, in earth as in heaven, like the church, the body of Christ, ruler of earth (through the emperor) as of heaven, the sage embodied what Israel was and was to be. So Israel as family in the model of the sage, like Moses our rabbi, corresponded in its social definition to the church of Jesus Christ, the New Israel, the source of salvation of the savior of humanity.

Do I think that Paul or Aphrahat will have accorded a sympathetic hearing to this theory of Israel, drawing Adam out of sin and upward at Sinai? or Israel as the suffering servant? of Israel as suffering for all humanity and its sins? No more than I should want to persuade the inestimable Nahmanides through arguments about how the Torah represents God in human form to listen more sympathetically to Christian talk about Jesus as God Incarnate. "In our image, after our likeness" may mean that we can ask, What would God be like, as a human being? It does not mean we must answer, *Ecce homo*. So, too, no Christian can concede that Israel at Sinai transformed the nature of humanity, as did Christ on the cross at Calvary; such would be nonsense talk, the opposite of dialogue. In the context of prior disputation, such talk is hopeless. Do I think that, reading the Torah, Nahmanides might find in the idea of divine pathos, or the sage in the image of God, a clue to what Christians might mean, how we might understand them, in talk about God Incarnate in Jesus Christ uniquely, alone and in particular? Yes, I do. In any event, I do. And I think that Paul in Romans 9 has tried to make sense, for himself in Christ, of his understanding of Israel, which is no different from that of the Torah in insisting upon Israel as God's planting. And the facticity of Isaiah, in speaking of Israel's fate in our own time and place, surely should move a Christian of today to not guilt but sympathy; of us it is truly said: "He was oppressed, and he was afflicted, yet he opened not his mouth; like a lamb that is led to the slaughter, and like a sheep that before its shearers is dumb, so he opened not his mouth."

Why do I think Christians should address this issue of "Israel" at all? Obviously, for the same reason that Christians themselves have asked about a dialogue with Judaism. In the aftermath of the Holocaust, Christians examined Christianity's doctrine of Israel, the Jews, and Judaism. Not responsible for the National Socialists—themselves anti-Christian—Christianity has come to recognize that Christians were National Socialists. While not the source of racist anti-Semitism, Christianity made its massive contribution to the racist anti-Semitism that formed the policy of mass murder of men, women, and children, in the name of the "purification" of humanity; and Christianity has come to recognize that theirs has been a teaching of contempt. But, prepared to enter into dialogue with Judaism, Christians have found the state of Israel an obstacle, and, I believe I have shown, that is for quite profound theological reasons.

First of all, though long experienced in governing, with a long history of a politically empowered church and a preference for Christian states, Christianity finds the notion of a Jewish state somehow egregious; religions do not have, or form, states (except, of course, rarely), so what can be Judaic about the state of Israel, so that Christianity, in addressing Judaism, should have to take notice also of the state of Israel? Second, the advent of the state of Israel really did call into question the theological convictions of many centuries. And, third, when we speak of "Israel," Judaic and Christian faithful really cannot concur that they speak of one and the same thing.

So much for the question. Can there be an answer? As I just said, to me, the words of Isaiah speak of us, not in long dark centuries past but in this very day:

> He was oppressed, and he was afflicted, yet he opened not his mouth; like a lamb that is led to the slaughter, and like a sheep that before its shearers is dumb, so he opened not his mouth.

To me, Isaiah describes my life and the life of my people: it is with me when I wake up in the morning and when I go to sleep at night. Can Christians tell our story in their way, so that they

may find sympathy for us? Clearly, they can, and many do. That
is why I do not doubt that Christians can find in the story of
Christ resources for telling themselves, also, the story of Israel
in our times. And in reading the suffering servant as we do,
they will discover for that conviction of ours that we are Israel,
after the flesh, after the spirit alike, the resources not for assent
but only for sympathetic hearing. Then, but only then, dialogue
with Judaism as it is, with us as we are and not with a fabrication of Christianity, can commence. We do our best with the
Incarnate God; now you try to do your best with Israel—and
no quotation marks this time.[1]

---

[1]In this context it is demeaning to say that I do not confuse religious dialogue with political expediency; I make no claim that for the
sake of dialogue, the Christian partner must then approve every deci-
sion of the most current Israeli government. Religious dialogue on
religious concerns, defined in a mutually comprehensible sense of the
word "religious," surely is to be attained. But I do think that Christians who hold Israel, the state, to that higher, and unattainable, standard or condemn the state of Israel in vile and hateful language—
looking for every chance to compare Israeli policy to German National Socialist policy or to invoke "the Holocaust" in criticizing Israeli actions—have no place in dialogue with self-respecting Jews.
These people are little more than anti-Semites. We recall Rubenstein's
remark, cited in chapter 3, note 1: "Jews alone of all the people in the
world are regarded as actors and participants in the drama of sin and
innocence, guilt and salvation, perdition and redemption."

Epilogue

9

What Is at Stake in the Judeo-Christian Dialogue: Beyond Relativism, Before Ecumenism; a Time for Storytelling

Neither Judaism nor Christianity finds itself prepared for theological dialogue, but a dialogue aimed at eliciting, each from itself, sympathy for profoundly particular and deeply held convictions of the other can only serve God's purpose, if each of us is prepared, along with Islam, to take seriously the possibility that one and the same God really has more than one and the same thing to say to the whole of humanity. Without asking ourselves specifically to say what we honestly believe God has to say in someone else's language to an utterly other, we may, I have argued, find resources in what we believe God has said to us to hear sympathetically the story of what God has said to that other. But why, in worldly terms, do I think it worth the effort?

It is because, through an earned increment of understanding, paid for out of one's own and not the other's treasure of godly truth, each of us may cope with a long-standing and acknowledged flaw. The beam in the eye of Christianity is, of course, its imperialism, amply illustrated in my representation of the Christian invention of Judaism, on the one side, and the Christian caricature of Israel, on the other.[1] The beam in my

---

[1]Chapters 2 and 4, respectively.

own eye, not so difficult to discern, is Judaic isolationism, not so much self-righteousness as standoffishness, which holds that God has given us 613 commandments, but to everybody else only 7. There is, after all, a certain pride in Amos's saying, "Only you have I known . . . therefore will I visit . . . ," and in our certainty that the dreadful things that have happened to us bear meaning, express a clear divine intent; other people just have disasters. God's love for the land, God's infinite concern for everything we do, the message of Leviticus 26 and Deuteronomy 32—these do spill over, perhaps quite naturally, into a certain isolationism: God cares what I eat for breakfast, but God cares only that you organize a just social order. God cares for me more than God cares for you. Perhaps that conclusion need not follow from the doctrine of "the seven commandments assigned to the children of Noah," meaning, everybody but us, but still, when I weigh 613 against 7, we do come out ahead.

Christianity really did bring the written Torah to the whole world. Christianity really did form the ideal of an entire civilization framed around the principles of the Torah, for instance, the Ten Commandments. Much that Jesus said[2] comes to him from the Torah, and still more will have pleased sages of his and later times, had they learned some of the fine things he said. Christian imperialism carries to an extreme the remarkable accomplishment of Christianity: along with imperial Islam, bringing knowledge of the Lord God, creator of heaven and earth, to the whole earth. We bear witness to the costs of that accomplishment, reminding the other to remember.

For our part, the prophet of the gentiles came to curse, as so many have done, but stayed to bless:

> For from the top of the mountains I see him,
>   from the hills I behold him;

---

[2]In the context of theological discourse, we need not say "much that is attributed to . . . ," and we cannot speak of much of Christianity and at the same time distinguish what he "really" said from what the church produced.

lo, a people dwelling alone,
and not reckoned among the nations!

Numbers 23:9

We have more than suffered and survived, we have risen from
the dead, we have endured. Coming out of the death camps
built to murder them, the survivors, along with Jewry throughout the world, had the option to take, each one, his or her own
way outward and away. After such horrors, who would want to
be a Jew, or who would want ever again to raise a child to be a
Jew? But that is not what happened. Most of Israel, the Jewish
people, joined with the tiny community then in the Land of
Israel to form, three years beyond Auschwitz, the state of Israel; and most of Israel, the Jewish people, determined to re-
new the life of Israel, not only the state in politics and the
people in the ethnic mosaic of the West but also, for more than
a few, that holy Israel whom God first loved. But in rising from
the grave, we too exact a price, first of all of ourselves: at what
cost? At all costs? These are the questions of a Christianity that
does not want to see us repeat the mistakes of Christianity.

If I see the stake of dialogue in terms of the end of Judaic
isolationism and Christian imperialism, that negative scarcely
suffices. I have a question to which Christianity may help find
answers. The Torah tells us that we are like God and, speaking
to Israel, requires us to be a kingdom of priests and a holy
people. How humanity may be like God, how a people, nation,
or community may become "a holy people"—these form questions addressed to the outer limits of imagination. Judaism,
Christianity, along with Islam—these three know God through
a revelation that, at its end, claims to form connections to the
beginning; Torah, Christ, Quran—all three are testimonies,
each in the eye of its beholder, to what God is like, therefore to
what God wants of us; to what the holy people is supposed to
be like, therefore to what God wants us to do together. For the
issue is not one of politics or sociology, it is a fundamental
question of what it means to love God, in particular the God
who has made himself known in the Torah, the Bible, and the

Quran, for all three of us claim that we are speaking of one and the same god, the One God.

Do Torah, Christ, and Quran speak to the same humanity? All three speak of living life under God, one God, the only God, the same God for us all. All three give testimony to a god that is sovereign and good. All three share fundamental assumptions, such as, in the words of Walter Moberly, "the dignity of human life, the centrality of love, trust, obedience, mercy, forgiveness; the living of the life of faith in community; prayer as the essential medium between God and humanity."[3]

Christians, Jews, Muslims respond, as deep calls to deep: we can respond to the poetry of the other, the yearning for God conveyed by the other, the love of God that nourishes the other. Should we lose all this, in the name of theological affirmation, with a merely down-home consequence? Having dismissed a discredited relativism but never opened the way to ecumenism, we undertake a small thing indeed: to find in the stories we tell ourselves the face and form of the other portrayed in the stories that the other tells too. Toward a Judeo-Christian dialogue of quest, each for a tale to tell the authentic humanity of the other, events of this awful century have brought us. It is time. And there is no other way.

---

[3]Personal letter, August 8, 1991.

General Index

Index of Biblical and Talmudic References